CUBA
A Story of Revival

RICHARD PARKER

ACW Press
Eugene, Oregon 97405

Cover design by Alpha Advertising
Interior design by Pine Hill Graphics

Packaged by ACW Press
85334 Lorane Hwy.
Eugene, Oregon 97405
www.acwpress.com
The views expressed or implied in this work do not necessarily reflect those of
ACW Press. Ultimate design, content, and editorial accuracy of this work is
the responsibility of the author(s).

Library of Congress Cataloging-in-Publication Data

Parker, Richard, 1951-
    Cuba : a story of revival / by Richard Parker. -- 1st.
  ed.
    p. cm.
    ISBN 1-892525-36-4

    1. Cuba--History--1959- 2. Missions--Cuba. 3. Cuba
--Church history. I. Title.

F1788.P37 2001   972.9106'4
                  QBI01-200181

This book is written to glorify our Lord and Savior Jesus Christ, the only living Son of God. It is my hope that the result of this work will be to help others find a tangible way in their lives to help fulfill the Lord's Great Commission. By building houses of worship in Cuba and around the world we can create a bridge to reach the unsaved for Christ.

—⋙— —⋙— —⋙—

"All authority in heaven and on earth has been given to me. Therefore go and make disciples of all nations baptizing them in the name of the Father and the Son and of the Holy Spirit, and teaching them to obey everything I have commanded you. And surely I am with you always, to the very end of the age."

Matthew 28:18-20

CONTENTS

DEDICATED IN LOVING MEMORY OF

Joshua Bryce Cole

9/18/95–2/16/98

This book is dedicated in memory of our grandson Joshua Bryce Cole. Josh was born on a warm September day in 1995. He had fiery red hair and at times a temper to match. He was my son Shane's only son and we all loved him as much as life itself. At three months old he played the part of baby Jesus in our church's Christmas play. Little did we know that less than two and one-half years later he would be with Jesus in heaven.

He was as inquisitive and full of energy as any two-year-old boy could ever be. Just before his death he had learned to say grace before our meals. He loved to do that so much, and at some meals wanted to bless every bite just to say "Amen," clap his hands together, rock back and forth in his highchair and smile with two-year-old pride.

Ever the big boy, he wanted to do everything himself. Whether it was opening doors, chewing gum, or climbing into his chair, he could do it all by himself. Barney was his favorite TV show and he was laid to rest with his Barney, his bottle and his Bible.

The cause of his death was never determined. His last night with us, his biggest concern was getting his bottle refilled before his Dad tucked his healthy and happy son into bed. As Josh left in the dark hours before dawn, he took with him a piece of us that can never be replaced. It is hard to understand why he was taken from us so young. In a recent message our pastor said, "God puts us all on this earth for a reason, and when that reason is fulfilled he takes us home." If I am fair, I must admit Josh's young life has already touched thousands.

This is the second book I have dedicated to him. Josh's death was the reason I took the time to write the first book, *Bible-Based Money Management™ Seminars (BBMMS)*. That book shows, from a Biblical perspective, how Christians should handle their money. It is now taught in hundreds of churches and to thousands of Christian families annually. In its first year in print, *BBMMS* was responsible for several million dollars of gifting to the Kingdom's work nationwide at the church level. Now, this second book, *Cuba: A Story of Revival*, will hopefully be the catalyst for building many churches in Cuba while impacting thousands of additional lives.

Josh, we all miss you, son, and I promise you that your young life did and does matter. We thank God for the time we had with you and now commend you into Jesus' hands to care for you until we can join you again at the throne of God.

ACKNOWLEDGMENTS

From the bottom of my heart I would like to thank the following friends, family and coworkers for their roll in the writing and production of this book. Just as a pebble dropped into a pond sends a ripple to every corner, who knows how far *Cuba – A Story of Revival* may reach because of your collective efforts.

Maybe this book will touch the heart of one person who will be lead to build a Church to honor a saintly parent. In that church, hundreds of people may receive the gift of eternal salvation. Perhaps that church will plant dozens of other churches across Cuba. With God all things are possible. No matter whether it is one soul or hundreds that are reached for the Lord, you should know that you played a valuable roll in this labor of love.

Several Staff members of my brokerage firm, Summit Brokerage Services, Inc. and Bible-Based Money Management™ Seminars were indubitably significant. To Suzanne "eagle-eye" Dubay, my executive assistant, who proofed the rough draft, as one of her first duties with the firm, and then proofed it again and again and again! To our resident "techies" Jeff Hopper and Amado Ohland who were always there with great attitudes. Thank you for preparing the photos and assisting with the graphics of the book as well as keeping the hardware and software up and running. To Rev. Chuck Newman and Chip Spear of Bible-Based Money Management™ Seminars and Mark Caulfield, Chief Financial Officer of Summit, for helping with my workload, which gave me the time to bring this to a successful completion. A million thanks to each one of you!

At International Cooperating Ministries many thanks go to Dois Rosser for his vision and leadership. He is a shining example of how a Christian Businessman can honor the Lord with his life. Also at ICM, Craig Falwell, Burt Reed and Jose Morelos, who did so much to assist with this project. From finding photos to accompanying us to Cuba, they were great. I will never forget Jose as he interpreted my emotional message at the dedication of Josh's church in old Havana. I would also like to thank another great man of God, Dick Woodward, Founder of the Mini-Bible College and an ICM partner. Finally, I would like to acknowledge my friend and Christian brother, Del Palmer, who, through his friendship, opened the doors that allowed me to meet and befriend all these fine men of God.

In my spiritual life, I wish to thank my pastors at Trinity Presbyterian Church, Rev. Michael Carey and Rev. Chris Romig whose weekly spiritual nourishment I always look forward to, especially upon returning from one of my all too frequent trips across this great country. I would also like to thank Rev. Chuck Magruder whose Bible study on "When Bad Things Happen to Good People" meant so much to me personally and to this book.

At ACW, our publisher, special thanks to Steve Laube and his staff for walking us through the publishing process.

Lastly, a heartfelt thanks to several of my family members. First my parents Rev. Richard & Doris Parker for giving me the loving Christian family to build a solid base upon and the patience to let me find my way back to the Lord. To Gale, my daughter-in-law, for loving and supporting my son Shane after Josh's death. We all love you so much. To my son Wayne for being a brother when Shane needed one, and, of course, to my partner in life, my wife Joan without whom I would not be the man I am today. You have loved me for over two decades, stood beside me and shared the ups and downs of our life. Darling, I thank God everyday for a Christian wife like you.

CHAPTER ONE

Preparing to Leave

The Big Day Arrives

As I awoke to the built-in alarm clock installed in my head at birth, I strained to peer through my sleep-filled eyes trying to focus on the night stand where the illuminated, red block numbers told me it was 5:49 A.M. I slowly emerged from beneath the covers on that April morning in 2000. By the dawn's early light it looked to be a normal Thursday morning in the Sunshine State of Florida. As my feet lightly touched the floor, I quickly realized this day's normality had two noticeable exceptions. The first was, this day had begun boasting of a record low temperature for that day of the year, set when a rapidly moving cold front plunged the temperatures to forty-two degrees in our sleepy hundred-year-old East Coast community of Melbourne Beach. A combination of the cool air temperature and the colder ceramic tile beneath my feet got my attention and started my blood pumping.

Within a moment of awakening, I remembered the second reason this day would be anything but a normal day. The end of this day would find my youngest son, Shane, along with fifteen other Christian men, and myself beginning our next bout with slumber in the island nation of Cuba, the last stronghold of communism in our hemisphere.

Elian's Story Hits Center Stage on the Wrong Day

As I began to make the morning coffee, I turned on one of the six televisions in our home, which we have grown to need much more than seems healthy. Half listening, as I struggled to separate the coffee filters, the morning news report suddenly caught my ear. I stopped my java preparation, increased the volume on T.V. number four and listened intently to the overnight developments in what had come to be daily coverage of the ongoing saga of the Cuban child, Elian Gonzalez. The six-year-old boy had been plucked from certain death in the Atlantic Ocean by Donato Dalrymple, a passing fisherman, as he clung to an inner tube on Thanksgiving Day, four months earlier. Elian was the only survivor from the hopeful but ultimately ill-fated voyage to freedom which claimed the lives of ten of his fellow Cuban exiles, including his mother. His bright-eyed face had become familiar in America, Cuba, and, in fact, the entire world.

The circumstances surrounding the rescue of this six-year-old had destined him to become a media event for the world. There were just too many points of interest for the media to let this story slip from the first page to the twelfth and then into obscurity. There was a young boy with dark, haunting eyes who had lost his mother as she desperately tried to reach America. There was also a custody battle not only between family members, but between the Cuban population of two countries who have had no love lost between them for over forty years. Add a Thanksgiving Day rescue, a couple dozen lawyers, and the U.S.

The most famous first grader in the world in 1999.

Justice Department—along with the day-and-night vigil from the Cuban-American population in Miami that had surrounded his temporary "Little Havana" home—and it was no wonder the media had locked on this like a hound dog treeing a raccoon.

Dad Arrives

For obvious reasons, I had a high degree of interest in that morning's news coverage. While my family and I were sleeping, the little boy's father, Juan Miguel Gonzalez, had left Cuba in the pre-dawn hours by private jet and had just, that hour, touched down in Washington, D.C. The father was accompanied by grandparents, doctors, and a small entourage of Cuban citizens, each vowing not to leave the United States without Juan's son. Rhetoric in both countries had escalated to new heights within the last forty-eight hours. It is impossible to discern if the primary motivation of one or both countries was helping Elian or achieving their own political agenda. What could not be denied was the fact that a six-year-old boy had lost his mother, and his only surviving parent was now in the United States demanding the child's return to Cuba.

Juan Michael Gonzalez, Elian's father

The United States, like it or not, had become the battleground for what was turning into a legal battle royal between the boy's Cuban-American great-uncle, Lazaro Gonzalez, who had been named as the temporary, court-appointed guardian, and his Cuban father. Shortly after the rescue, Janet Reno, Attorney General of the United States, had gone on record stating that the U.S. Government's position was to let the drama play out in the courts. By January, this "let the courts decide" U.S. government stance had been replaced with a call, by Reno's office, to return the boy to his father. In almost any circumstance, most people would agree that having lost one parent, it was in the child's best interest to be returned to the only surviving parent, in this case, his father Juan Miguel.

Little Havana's Not Happy with Big Havana

But in the complex world in which we live, this decision was not as simple as it seemed on the surface. The Cuban-American population is located primarily in three communities in the United States: Union City, New Jersey; Tampa, Florida; and Miami, Florida. Miami is the home to the largest contingency with over one million Cuban-Americans living in an area known as "Little Havana." Putting it mildly, "Little Havana" had strong feelings about giving Elian back to "Big Havana," and, more specifically, they saw it as giving the boy to Fidel Castro himself. From their viewpoint, the mother had died in the process of bringing her son to America, and therefore he should be allowed to stay. Now, after four months, it looked as though the courts were about to rule in favor of returning the child to his father.

My Boyhood Memories

Cuba is located only ninety miles from the United States' southern-most city, the pristine Key West, Florida. Key West has been the last American stop—or the first depending on your latitude of destination—for Americans and Cubans for many decades. This was to be my first trip to the closest Communist country to my homeland.

I still have a vivid memory of growing up as a fifth-generation Floridian in the East Coast city of Fort Pierce, located an hour and a half south of the Kennedy Space Center and two and a half hours north of Miami. Fort Pierce was more a sleepy cow town than a city in the 1960s, with its major industries focused on growing oranges and raising cattle.

In 1962, I was an eleven-year-old, impressionable boy whose world, at that time, revolved around tree houses and tire swings. I can still recall when the word *Cuba* first entered my limited childhood vocabulary.

I remember sitting under a century-old, live oak tree with tangles of moss blowing in the warm Florida breeze like the beard of a wise old southern gentleman. As I sat there in the late afternoon on the east side of the railroad tracks, originally laid by Henry Flagler in his quest to connect New York to Key West, I peered west. With boyhood inquisitiveness, I sat shielding my eyes from the strobe light effects of the setting sun as it flashed between railroad cars of yet another endless troop train headed South. I was still too young to fully appreciate the horrific danger that loomed just off the Florida coast only 400 miles to the south of my seemingly safe and protected boyhood home.

Few thoughts occupied my mind for very long in those days. Most centered around whether or not the fish were biting, if I had enough change in the pockets of my cut-off jeans for a Coke and a bag of peanuts, and, more recently, around a pretty ten-year-old girl with blond hair and bright blue eyes whom I had known for years but had just begun to truly appreciate.

Just Over the Horizon

The island nation of Cuba is nestled in the Caribbean Sea located less than one hundred miles west of Haiti and just over one hundred miles north of Jamaica. As I sat by the railroad tracks in the early 1960s, little did I know that some twenty years later the island of Jamaica would serve as the tropical setting in which I would wed my wife, Joan, long after the threat of World War III had become a distant, bad memory.

Cuba seems to float in the emerald green water south of the Florida Straits, like a glistening jewel. Crops of tobacco, used in its world-famous cigar industry, grow well in the lush country-side. For years prior to the late 1950s, the casinos of Cuba welcomed tourists from around the world seeking sun, fun, and an array of legalized vices.

The Crisis

On May 29th, 1962, the USSR through its leader Nikita S. Khrushchev reached an agreement with Cuba to deploy medium-range and intermediate-range missiles. In August of 1962 the deployment of forty-two medium-range nuclear missiles began with the assignment of a group of IL-28 Soviet medium-range bombers and a 43,000-strong Soviet military contingent to Cuba. The American intelligence community suspected that missiles were being deployed but had no proof. When questioned, the Soviet leader assured America that no missiles were being placed on Cuban soil.

Then in late September of 1962 an over-flight of western Cuba, by a United States U-2 spy plane, brought back photos of

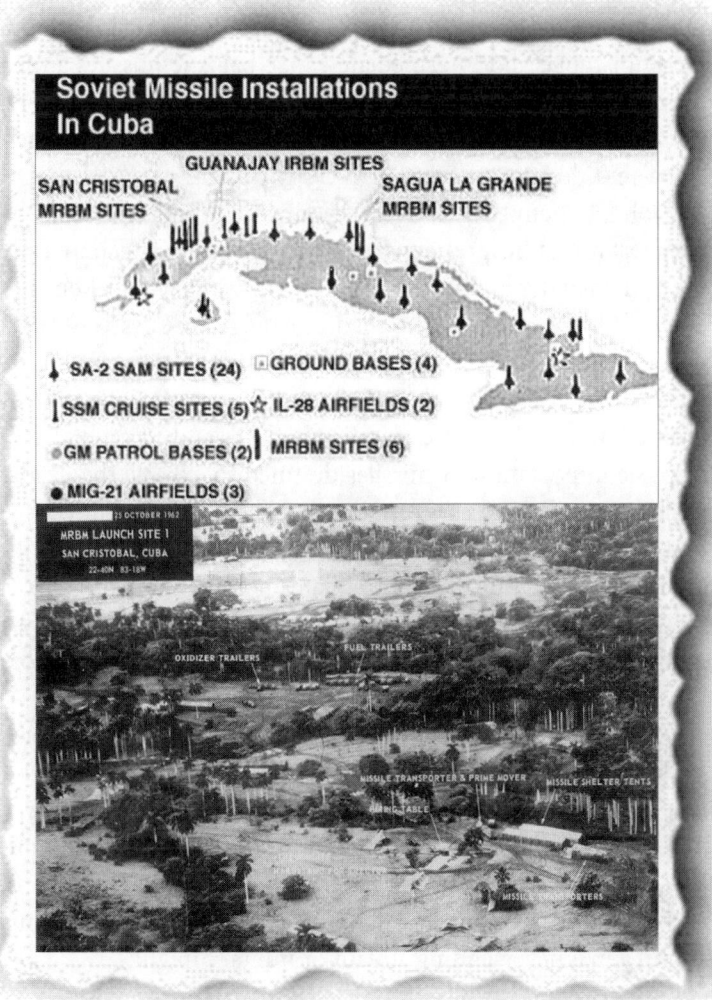

Kennedy's proof—A photo taken in September 1962 from an American U-2 spy plane of a Cuban Launch Site. This site proves to be one of many with US strike capability as shown on the map at top.

a trapezoidal pattern characteristic of Soviet missile installations. There was now no denying that Cuba, an ally of the Soviet Union, America's long-time arch rival, was being converted to a nuclear arsenal, with its deadly warheads carried by both medium-range and intermediate-range ballistic missiles aimed primarily at the United States. Tensions further escalated when on October 27, 1962, a Cuban anti-aircraft battery in Banes, Cuba shot down an American U-2 spy plane.

John F. Kennedy, America's youngest president, faced the toughest test of his presidency—a test that could affect not only the United States and Russia but humanity as a whole. Kennedy knew that the range of the medium-range missiles was 1,100 nautical miles and the intermediate missiles had a range that reached over 2,000 miles. The young American president ordered a naval blockade to encircle the island in an effort to stop the importation of missiles destined to expand the deadly nuclear arsenal. For years America had lived with the knowledge that the Soviets had targeted our country, and we theirs, with enough nuclear punch to annihilate most of the world. Now there was the alarming reality of knowing it would take only a matter of minutes for a Soviet missile—based in Cuba—to cross the Straits of Florida and reach American soil.

As the world held its breath this surreal game of *super-power chicken* continued. What would happen? Would the world end in a series of bright atomic flashes? To an eleven-year-old boy, a more realistic threat seemed that South Florida would sink into the Atlantic Ocean from the sheer weight of the tanks, troops, and military hardware headed to the smaller latitudes of our country in a never-ending stream of military might.

Presidential Priorities—Cohibas

Thank God the missile crisis passed! However, the United States embargo, begun in 1962, continues into the twenty-first century—much longer than either side thought it would last.

Pierre Slazenger, Press Secretary to President Kennedy, tells a humorous story of the embargo's beginning. After the decision to set the blockage was reduced to paper, the president called

Slazenger into his office and told him to obtain 1,000 Cuban cigars for him and to let him know when the task was complete. When Slazenger reported that he had procured 1,200 Cohibas, Kennedy thanked him, then pulled the blockade documents from his desk drawer and signed them. I am sure neither side foresaw that almost forty years later the embargo would remain, upheld now by seven American presidents.

We, as a country, have steadfastly refused to lift economic sanctions against Cuba. The results of that decision, or more precisely the lack of a decision to cease the embargo, is viewed by some Americans as good; others disagree. The devastating results of the embargo, coupled with the many poor economic decisions made by the Castro regime, are apparent the moment you clear Customs in that island nation.

Should We Still Go?

That brisk, April 6 morning, I began to seriously question the timing of our trip to Cuba. Would we face problems? Would we be targeted as unwelcome American capitalists? I could see visions of our aging van being rocked from side to side by an angry anti-American mob intent on inflicting injury or even death on the handiest example of the United States—us. Was I walking into—and, more importantly, was I leading my son into—harms way?

I began that departure morning in the solitude of my home office, with my daily devotional and a prayer, asking God to give me the wisdom to make the right decisions. Should I postpone our trip or leave that day as planned? The determination was made that we would proceed with our mission trip. I was traveling with a group of seventeen Christian businessmen whose goal was to increase the number of Christian churches on the island. As I finished my morning devotional, I then prayed for strength, guidance and safety for my son, my fellow travelers, and myself on the journey.

Wheels Down—He's Here

Our flight was not scheduled to leave until mid day, which allowed me a leisurely morning at home prior to our departure for the airport. Blaring from all six televisions in our home, the coverage of the Elian battle continued. At about 9:00 A.M. Juan Gonzalez stepped out of the Lear Jet and on to the tarmac of a Washington, D.C. airport. He stepped to the cluster of microphones placed at the podium and withdrew a prepared speech from his inside coat pocket. Tentatively at first but then with growing forcefulness, he began to address the world. Knowing his words would be simultaneously broadcast around the globe, he began to relate his feelings of being separated from his son for the past four months. He reprimanded the United States government for its refusal to allow his son to leave America for the previous one-third of a year. He demanded an immediate release so that he and Elian could immediately return to Cuba, and he pledged that, no matter how long it took, he would remain in the United States until the child was allowed to return with him to their homeland.

After a ten-minute speech, being translated by a Cuban-provided interpretor, a diplomat of Cuba then stepped to the podium. He stated that while Juan and his fellow Cubans remained in the United States, the Cuban residence where they would be staying would waive diplomatic immunity. I did not immediately understand the implications of this. In the commentary after the speeches it was pointed out that by waiving immunity, the Cuban government was saying Juan and the other Cubans were free to move about the country, and if they returned to Cuba they were returning of their own free will. The Cuban-American leaders in Miami immediately rebutted this point. They stated no matter what steps were taken to convince the world that these Cuban visitors were free, in reality none of them had the choice of deciding to stay in the United States without creating problems for their families still remaining in

Cuba. Regardless of which side was true, this was the backdrop for our trip to Cuba, scheduled to begin in less than three hours.

Wheels Up—We're Gone

Still, a degree of apprehension was in the air as my wife and my daughter-in-law, Gale, drove my son Shane and myself to the Orlando International Airport. After bidding farewell, we boarded the American Eagle ATR42 which flew southeast to the east coast of Florida. When we reached Vero Beach, just fifteen miles south of our beachfront home, we turned east and headed over the rapidly moving Gulf Stream to our first stop—Nassau, Bahamas.

Our group had received special permission, as a humanitarian effort, from the U.S. Government for our trip to Cuba. Our flight was filled with a combination of Bohemians returning home, focused and busy businessmen, and vacationers clad in Bermuda shorts along with several obviously excited gamblers ready to try their luck at the tables of Nassau. On a daily basis hundreds of gamblers make the short trip from the Florida East Coast by plane or boat to the legalized gambling of the Bahamas. Many carry little or no luggage as they have planned to return on the last flight of the day, tired and hopefully, but not usually, a bit richer. Within ninety minutes we touched down on the coral island, surrounded by the beautiful turquoise water known for its plentiful supply of grouper, cobia, snapper and dolphin.

CHAPTER TWO

Nassau

Nassau—I Spent 7 Years
There One Morning

After taxiing to the terminal, we deplaned to the tarmac where we were greeted by the blast of humidity the tropics are famous for. As we entered the semi-modern terminal, I could not help but notice the collage of missing ceiling tiles that create a checker-board appearance overhead. I then read the sign over the door welcoming us to the Commonwealth of the Bahamas. Inside the airport, the country's official welcoming band of the day, "The Bohemian Gang," filled the air with the sounds of steel drums. As "The Bohemian Gang" sang a song of fish, sun, and rum we were herded, cattle-style, through customs, while official signs reminded us not to smoke, have our paperwork ready, and, above all, stand clearly behind the infamous yellow line. We watched a two-year-old boy with Shirley Temple curls dance his own version of the Mambo, while his mother and father looked on adoringly. The family appeared to have also brought Grandma along on the family vacation, most likely to give Mom and Dad some time for Nassau's night life. Curly boy, announcing to everyone his age with two fingers held in front of his nose, brought smiles to the faces of the passengers waiting in line. As a musical backdrop to the pint-size floorshow, "The Bohemian Gang" played a song that strongly resembled the "Sloop John B."

Don't Smile, You May Lose Your Job

All attempts at small talk with the stone-faced custom officials failed. As the purple ink dried on my passport, I was directed to the luggage search area. As we prepared to unpack our five-day supply of underwear, socks, and snacks, we were waved through with a gesture so ornate it could have been invented at the Vatican. So much for Nassau's tight security! I reasoned that the Bohemian government is willing to take a calculated risk of contraband entering the country, in favor of the speed in which they hustle the gamblers to their donation positions at the country's blackjack and craps tables.

As the members of our seventeen-man group began assembling in the terminal, we were told that if by some unlikely event our plane to Cuba departed on time, we still would have another two and a half hours until our departure.

The Famed Mel Gibson

My son and I conducted a quick negotiation with a taxi driver who introduced himself as Mel Gibson. "Like the actor, mon," he proudly stated, although the business card in the candy dish located in the passenger compartment of his aging limousine displayed the name of Derek Gibson. Oh well, Mel was an easy name to remember and he obviously enjoyed hearing it. So for an agreed upon price of $50 (U.S.) he placed his demolition-derby-style island tour into full forward motion. Mel assured us we would return no later than 3:15 P.M. for our 4:00 P.M. flight.

The famous Mel Gibson's limousine

"Besides, mon," he stated, "De flights all run on Bahamas time. Not much chance she takes off before 4:00. We all take our time in de islands." I can assure you that a truer statement has never been spoken. The rear tires of Mel's white limo caught a patch of sand in front of the airport and give a squeal announcing the beginning of our memorable journey to downtown Nassau.

Let's Do Lunch—Island Style

Early in our roadway tour we asked our jovial and animated driver to stop for a quick lunch, either on our way to or from the town, while an English menu could still be found. He informed us that he knew just the place and the food was great. Enough said on the topic, our lunch plans had now been placed in the capable hands of the famed Mel Gibson. He was most willing to share his local knowledge at no additional charge as we left the airport in our rearview mirror. Mel quickly looked over his shoulder and said, "Don't worry, mon, I know all de best eating establishments on the island. We will have a great lunch." Excited about our upcoming island-cuisine lunch, we issued an invitation for him to join us, which he gladly accepted.

In a few minutes we reached downtown Nassau, with its clean and crisp century-old colonial architecture. Mel pulled the two-football-field long limousine into a "No Parking Zone" then announced, in a joyous voice, "We are here, mon." As he opened his door, Shane and I looked from left to right. We both began to chuckle as we saw Mel making a beeline to the front door of the Wendy's fast food restaurant. Mel held the door open, bending slightly at the waist, as we approached the door. He suggested that he stay at the car in case one of the walking patrols of the helmeted Bohemian police, in their starched white jackets, should pass taking notice of our occupation of the clearly marked "No Parking Zone." "I'll take a chicken nugget special," he announced as we entered the restaurant. So much for island delicacies.

And They're Off

After enjoying our over-extended tour of both old downtown Nassau and the new beach resort area with its multi-story casinos, Mel Gibson displayed his talent of dodging on-coming traffic while alternating his attention between the steering wheel and the horn.

Mel finally came to a screeching stop, worthy of any *Lethal Weapon* movie scene, in front of the airport door. We parted with a smile, a handshake, and a promise to call only Mel on our future trips to the Commonwealth of the Bahamas. Sensing the urgency of time, we walked as fast as our wobbling legs could carry us to our departure gate, fighting the urge to stop, kiss the ground and give thanks for our safe return. What a ride, mon!

Hurry Up and Wait

Like the thirteen people in front of me, I, too, set off the alarm on the 1970s model metal detector we passed through to reach our gate. Each of us waited patiently as our limbs were swept with what appeared to be the island's only hand-held metal-detection unit. We were then motioned unceremoniously to proceed to our gate.

As the airline employee behind the desk drifted sleepily in and out of consciousness, we again tested our ability to wait patiently. That day we were lucky and began boarding our Canadian Aerogaviota ART42 less than one hour after our scheduled departure time. The boarding process completed, we sat in ninety-degree heat for the customary thirty minutes or until all passengers are soaked to the bone, whichever is longer.

CHAPTER THREE

Cuba Now and Then

Our Flight to Cuba

As we began climbing to our 19,000-foot cruising altitude, we bade a fond farewell to the Commonwealth of the Bahamas. I stole a glance from the starboard-side window of our plane and believed I could barely make out a very long, aging, white limo passing three cars and barely making it back to the left lane only seconds before a head-on collision. I settled into my very worn seat, laid my head back, closed my eyes and smiled knowing that some island tourist with white knuckles was being introduced to the sights of Nassau, Bahamas by none other than the famed Mel Gibson, "like the actor, mon."

The hour-and-twenty-minute flight to Cuba flew by in what seemed like only four and a half hours. It is amazing how much we, as Americans, have come to expect being protected from the obvious. I was surprised to see two Cuban gentlemen neatly stack several large boxes in front of the exit door of our plane. The flight attendant seemed not to mind the placement of the boxes and saw no need for the standard seat belt announcement. I am sure she, like most seasoned travelers, felt no need for a quick lesson on the working parts of the seat belt buckle. Then the obviously unhappy, or at least bored, young flight attendant began handing out your choice of iceless, lukewarm Coke, equally warm beer or Cuba Libra, in small plastic cups. The drinks were accompanied with a packaged product, which looked like a semi-colorless Cheeto but tasted like nothing I'd ever consumed in my lifetime. After two bites—the second only to assure myself that my taste buds had not misled me—I ceased my consumption. My thoughts turned to the many starving children my mother had reminded me of while growing up. I then decided to save the colorless, tasteless corn product in case I saw any of those children on this trip. On second thought, I decided to throw them away. No one should give this food product (using the broadest definition of the word food) to another human being on purpose.

Land Ho

Just after 6:00 P.M. we crossed the eastern coast of the island of Cuba and prepared for our landing at Holguín Airport. While peering out the window of the plane, I observed that the beach, in this section of Cuba, is unlike most beach areas in Florida. There's no gaggle of high-rise condominiums and no bumper-to-bumper traffic. There is no flashing neon beckoning you to lay down your Cuban pesos for fast food, quick fun and cheap lodging. From the air you can see miles of undeveloped, sandy beaches. I can not help but think what a diamond-in-the-rough most American developers would see in Cuba. This beach area abuts, quite unceremoniously, the clearly recognizable agricultural squares which denote a farming community. Small hamlets dot the landscape of the tropical island. Few roads, mostly dirt, dissect the countryside. But the agricultural impact to the Cuban economy is clear even at our 5,000-foot altitude.

The Revolution Years

The terrain on our initial approach to the airport is flat, much like Florida, but the mountainous area Montañés de Nipe-Sagua Baracoa, can be viewed on the horizon. These mountains fade into the Sierra Maestra Mountains to the south. I later learned that these mountains which extend north of Guantánamo and past Santiago de Cuba once served as home for a young lawyer, and revolutionary named Fidel Castro. It was in Santiago de Cuba that on July 26, 1953 Castro led a band of 131 revolutionaries in the infamous and ill-fated raid on the Moncada military barracks. This was the first major attempt to overthrow the dictator, General Fulgencio Batista. When the revolutionaries lost the element of surprise, the battle quickly deteriorated for them. Faced with certain defeat, Castro ordered a retreat to the mountains.

Only 18 of the 131 escaped death or capture. For a week the remaining small band would hide in the higher parts of the mountain range. Day after day they kept on the move to avoid capture by government troops which continuously dogged them. The rag-tagged prelude to a revolutionary army, that would in less than six years topple the government, was now without food or water and most were at the point of total exhaustion. On the night of August 1, 1953, as they slept in a mountain jungle clearing, the small band was surprised by a squad of Cuban regulars commanded by second lieutenant, Pedro Manuel Sarria. All eighteen were arrested.

Fidel Castro's trial began on September 21, 1953. Castro, a lawyer by training, defended himself. By all accounts, the young lawyer gave a stirring defense, many times quoting the works of Jose Marti, a well-known Cuban patriot. Despite his efforts to defend himself, he and his fellow revolutionaries' actions subsequently earned him fifteen years in the Model Prison on the then Isle of Pines (today Isle of Youth.)

However, on May 15, 1955 Castro and the other assailants of the raid on the Moncada barracks were released by Batista. This would prove to be the Batista regime's worst mistake. Increasingly, for the next four and a half years, the rebel army led by Fidel, his brother Raul, Che Guevara, Juan Almeda, Camilo Cienfuegos and the only woman in the Revolutionary inner circle, Celia Sánchez, forged an uprising. The revolution culminated on New Year's Eve of 1959 when Batista transferred the leadership of the armed forces to General Eulogio Cantillo. That same day he resigned the presidency and, along with his top aides, fled the country.

Centuries of Struggle

One who studies Cuban history is reminded that it has for centuries been an island of struggle. Cuba is located in an area near the Tropic of Cancer. It is the largest island located in the Caribbean Sea or the Sea of Antilles and sits at the entry of the Gulf of Mexico. For this reason, Cuba is sometimes referred to as the Key to the Gulf.

The Lay of the Land

Cuba is divided into fourteen provinces with 169 municipalities, one of which is the Isle of Youth. The Isle of Youth is subordinated to the central government of Cuba. The provinces in Cuba are Pinar del Rio, the western-most Havana, Havana City, Matanzas, Cienfuegos, Villa Clara, Sancti Spíritus, Ciégo de Avila, Camagüey, Las Tunas, Holguín, Granma, and Santigo de Cuba. The eastern-most Guantánamo is still home to a large U.S. Naval base.

Cuba has a population of over eleven million people as of its most recent tabulation, conducted in January 1996. Demographically, 59 percent of the Cubans live in urban areas. It has a demographic density of 99 inhabitants per square kilometer. Approximately 66 percent of Cubans are white; 12 percent are blacks; 21.9 percent are mixed; and 0.1 percent are of Asian background. Cuba has ten cities whose population exceeds

100,000. The largest is Havana, the capital of the country, with 2,172,400 people. Cuba's constitution, in effect since 1976, establishes that Cuba is a socialist state of workers and peasants.

The country enjoys a semi-tropical climate with an almost constant cool sea breeze. One could say that Cuba enjoys a state of permanent summer. The country itself boasts of a rich variety of hardwoods and lush vegetation that covers the vast majority of the island. The most representative tree in the Cuban landscape is the royal palm. This beautiful and tall palm has a captivating beauty and a strong tropical appearance. When flying into the island you see thousands of them resembling clusters of gigantic seventy- to ninety-foot natural umbrellas. This stately palm with its gracefully curving trunk grows in all regions of Cuba. It is estimated that Cuba is home to over seventy million palms of all types. The national flower is the butterfly jasmine, but the island is home to more than 300 varieties of native orchids.

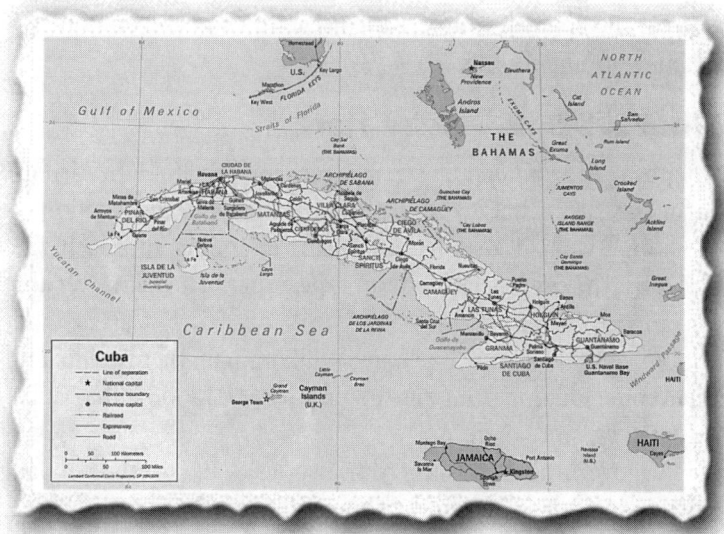

Cuba and its Caribbean neighbors

In 1492 Columbus Sailed the Ocean Blue

Christopher Columbus, an experienced sailor from Genoa who set sail on August 3, 1492, in three ships, the *Nina*, the *Pinta* and the *Santa Maria*, discovered Cuba as his second landfall. Columbus had sailed for seventy-two days when his crew grew increasingly restless, even to the point of mutiny. They feared that Columbus had gone insane as he pressed on relentlessly in search of the New World. On October 12, 1492, Andalucian sailor, Rodrigo de Triana, sighted land. Columbus's willpower and navigational skills had paid off. They had landed in the Bahamas. Columbus named the islands San Salvador since finding them in the nick of time saved him and his expedition from certain disaster.

While conversing with the natives mainly through sign language and gestures, Columbus learned that there was more land over the horizon and continued his voyage to the south. Fifteen days later on October 27, Columbus arrived at the coast of Cuba, which he named *Juana* in honor of Prince Juan, the first-born of the Spanish couple, King Fernando and Queen Isabel of Spain, who underwrote his voyage.

Wheels Down—We're Here

After our plane landed, my first glimpse of the Holguín Airport surprised me. In stark contrast to the slum-type construction of the homes we had just seen on our final landing approach, the Holguín Airport had a modern appearance. The sign over the entrance showed a huge portrait of Fidel Castro and announced—Welcome, Welkom, Willkommen, Bienvenido and Bienvenue. Judging from this first impression I took it that Cuba was glad we were there.

A government bus then transported us to the Cuban Customs area. The building, although older in construction, was very clean and had recently been painted. I soon discovered this was about the last fresh paint we were to find on the island.

Again we were greeted with the familiar "stand behind the line" signs although the color of the line had now changed from Nassau yellow to Cuban red. Initially I had a sense that the customs agents must have taken the same home-study course on maintaining a stone-faced countenance that their Nassau counterparts had completed. From all outward appearances, the Cubans graduated at the head of their class. Not a smile could be traced on any of their faces, and we were given glances that seemed to underline their untrusting outlook on foreigners—especially Americans.

We're Not in Kansas Anymore

After my third pass that day through an airport metal detector, all three in different countries, our group began to informally congregate in the baggage claim area. This area kept us separated from the Cuban people who stood on the outside of the building awaiting the arrival of friends and loved ones.

The many faces of Cuba

An army of baggage handlers were poised, ready to assist with carrying luggage from the terminal to the cars, taxis and tour busses parked in the patched but paved parking lot. Thick fixed-glass panels on all sides of the terminal separated the arriving passengers from the outside world. Lining the terminal windows were the faces—for the first time we saw the faces of the Cuban people. The older faces in the crowd silently told stories of decades of hard living conditions. But then there were the Cuban children. They were happy, alert, and smiling, no different than children found anywhere around the world. They looked at us through dark eyes filled with wide-eyed innocence and high expectation.

I noticed a Cuban family with several children, from the approximate ages of three to seven, standing in stair-step fashion. Having a soft spot in my heart for children, I began making gestures and playing with one little girl about five years old. Her little face was pressed tightly against the glass window that separated us. She reminded me of a kid in a candy store looking at the treats, which she knew she had no chance of actually receiving.

Tourist Apartheid

In recent years the Cubans have embraced tourism as a way to attract foreign currency. In the process, they have created a type of tourist-apartheid—a distinct separation of the haves (the tourist) and the have-nots (the Cuban people). The government has taken care to create areas and resorts where the tourists are catered to and made to feel safe. Noticeably absent from these areas are the local people. While Cubans, of course, provide the labor at these resorts and tourist areas, if for no other reason than money (or the lack thereof), none of the Cuban population, at large, are to be found mingling with the tourist. Considering the basic cornerstone of socialism is that all workers are equal, it seems quite a contradiction in thinking, but one that is, at least on the surface, willingly accepted by both the government and the Cuban population.

Hey Gringo Come with Me

So enthralled was I with playing with the little girl on the other side of the thick airport glass that I did not notice the two Cuban Customs agents who approached me from behind. For some reason, still unknown to me, they selected me and only me from our group. The first agent asked for my passport then ordered me to get my bags and follow them. Unsure of the reason I was being singled out from our group, but not wanting to create a problem in my first thirty minutes in the country, I grabbed my bags and followed their quick pace to a side area. As I walked away I glanced back nervously at my group, all of whom now ceased their conversations and stared helplessly as I was led away. I knew I had done nothing wrong. I was carrying no contraband, and, before I left the States, I had searched my bags, piece by piece, to make certain nothing could mistakenly cause a problem. I was hopeful I was only the first of our whole group to make this routine journey. I reasoned that this was probably just standard operating procedure, but the feeling in my stomach did not agree at all. I was led to a group of search tables and the interrogation began.

In broken English I was asked several questions that should have been easy to answer, but I was traveling with a group (International Cooperating Ministries (ICM), and the management of that group had made all the arrangements. As of yet, we had not had the time for a group meeting to share all the details of the next few days. All I really knew was that this was a mission trip to Cuba to dedicate some churches and to view other church sites that needed to be built. As the Cuban officials began questioning me, I grew increasingly uneasy because of my inability to answer even the simplest of questions. Each "I don't know" I uttered was met with raised eyebrows and more interest from an increasing number of Cuban Customs agents.

The questions on the surface sounded simple enough and had I been versed in the details of our trip, they would have been.

"Where are you staying?"

"I do not know," I replied.

As I tried to explain, both my lack of Spanish and the agent's broken English continued to get in the way. Another agent asked, "What is your means of transportation in Cuba?"

"I'm not sure," I answered.

"Will you be traveling to more than one city?"

"Yes, I will," I said, with a smile as I nodded in the affirmative, happy I could finally answer at least one question. Maybe the tide was turning I thought, but that was not to be the case. Just as the words left my mouth, my smile began to sink along with my heart as I anticipated their next obvious question.

"What cities will you be traveling to?" a rather large and impatient supervisor asked.

"Again, I do not know," I heard myself say with an almost out-of-body feeling. This reply was met with one agent throwing up his arms in an exasperated gesture and slowly turning 360 degrees. Even without a commanding knowledge of Spanish, I instinctively knew this was not going well.

Where is Everybody Going?

I then turned to see if I could get some help from my group. To my horror, I saw the entire group heading to the buses in the parking lot. I was being left in a Communist country and I could not even pinpoint on the map where I was, much less where we were going. Now I was getting scared.

At that moment I saw all nine agents, who were questioning me, turn in unison to view a Cuban newscast on one of two televisions mounted on the terminal walls.

I've Seen This Movie Before

While I could not understand the words, this was the same CNN news clip I had seen earlier that day of Juan Miguel Gonzalez, the father of Elian, as he read the defiant statement denouncing the United States for holding his son the past four months. All work ceased at the customs table as all the agents intently watched the newscast. Several short and obviously bitter statements were made to one another as I waited.

Open Mouth Insert Foot

Suddenly the newscast was over. Now the group of nine agents turned their full attention back to me. The ranking officer asked, "Where are you from?"

"The United States."

"Where in the United States?" he continued with even less patience. The feeling in my stomach grew more uncomfortable.

"Florida," I replied.

Two of the customs agents then replied in unison, "Miami!"

"No," I assured them, "Melbourne Beach." Never was I so glad that my home was not in South Florida. My next words were a pure stumbling masterpiece of oration. "You know," I said, "Just south of Kennedy Space Center." Then several of the agents nodded in the affirmative, saying in unison, "Si, we know *Kennedy*." I am sure the only thing that came to the agents' minds when I said "Kennedy" was The Bay of Pigs or the Missile Crisis. This thing was going from bad to worse.

Here Comes the Cavalry

Suddenly the only interpreter for our group appeared at my side. A couple of brief conversations in their native tongue seemed to calm the fears of the group of agents. They then began to disburse one by one. I was handed my passport and in broken English ordered to "enjoy your stay in Coo-bah." Then almost as an afterthought and, I guess, to prove that they, too, had a sense of humor, the big burly supervisor said, "Try not to get lost wherever you are going in Coo-bah," which was met with a round of laughter from the agents. I, too, gave a nervous laugh but did not let that get in the way of making a hasty retreat to the parking lot to board the bus which was, thankfully, still waiting for me to rejoin our group. Upon entering the bus I was met with smiles, questions and pats on the back. Like the returning conqueror the bus was alive with chatter. I was just glad it was beginning to roll towards the open road.

The Sweet Smell of Freedom

I never really knew how important the word *freedom* was until that moment. I had never really lost my freedom, but in that few minutes the inability to effectively communicate—coupled with the international tension created by the little dark-eyed Cuban boy's tug-of-war in Miami—made me glad to be leaving the Holguín Airport. Even though I did not know where I was going or how I was getting there, I was just glad to be on my way.

CHAPTER FOUR

Stepping Back in Time

The Time Capsule

We boarded our buses and began our one-hour ride to Playa Guardalavaca. As soon as we turned on the highway I noticed several things. First, unlike Nassau, we were driving on the right side of the road—that felt good within itself. It also seemed as if we had stepped back in time. Almost magically we were transported into what could easily be a Hollywood movie set of an old movie. Ancient Detroit sedans—Fords, Chevrolets and Dodges—were everywhere, many in surprisingly great shape for half-century-old automobiles. Since the embargo began, no automobiles from the world's largest producer of gas-guzzlers (the United States) have been exported to Cuba. Coupled with an average monthly income for Cuban workers of less than twelve dollars (U.S.), the hope of new car ownership seems all but an elusive, fleeting dream.

Even if a Cuban somehow managed to find the pesos to purchase the car, had Uncle Sam tipping his stovepipe hat to resuming exportation while the Boards of Directors from the Big Three automakers collectively sang the "Star Spangled Banner," a permit from the government would still be required before the purchase could be made. Some professions such as actors, professional athletes, and a few others have the ability to purchase automobiles. Government officials and military leaders are also allowed to purchase automobiles. Do not try to make sense out of salsa logic. As with many aspects of Cuban laws, logic is not part of the equation.

Detroit's Fifty-Year Cars

Prior to the 1959 revolution, the island of Cuba was a vacation paradise for the world. It was influenced greatly by the United States' politics and businesses. This is why so many vintage American vehicles still sputter down the pothole-filled, sun-baked roads. The other reason so many cars of yesteryear are found is the simple, reliable design of these post-World War II cars. At that point, Motor City offered few options on its assembly-line family cars. It was not until later that American ingenuity brought to market such luxuries as power steering, air conditioning, or elaborate electronic systems. Therefore, without these options, most cars simply had fewer parts to wear out. Adding even more to the longevity of the island's clunker population is the slow speed everyone travels, mostly due to the poor quality of the roads. Traffic almost always moves under 50 mph and usually between 30 and 45 mph. Cubans have lived for decades with a lack of replacement parts and fuel shortages, while importation of replacement vehicles is all but non-existent. When a car is eventually declared un-repairable, the Cubans literally scavenge every component of that car to keep other vehicles on the road. You will find no junkyards in Cuba. The Cubans are still driving their junkyards.

Cuba's transportation is frozen in time.

Dependence on Oil

The Soviets hooked the island on oil. In a short time Cubans craved oil like a drug addict craves the next fix. Oil dependence, as with a drug dependence, creates a very unpleasant reaction when withdrawal is forced, cold turkey. The Soviets addicted the Cubans when trading their oil for Cuban sugar. Cuba then built its industry around Soviet oil and machinery. After the collapse of the USSR, Cuba became a semi-modern country powered by ox carts. Along the rural roads, hundreds of peasants chop thousands of acres of sugarcane, one stalk at a time, and load it by hand on wooden carts drawn by oxen. Cuba has in retrospect, paid a heavy price for its ties with the USSR.

The Cuban Economy

After the collapse of the USSR, the Cuban government declared a "special period in peacetime." In essence, this was a wartime condition during peacetime. The break up, which happened in only three short years in the early 1990s, cost Cuba 75 percent of its imports and 95 percent of the foreign market for its exports, mainly its crops. Since the USSR was Cuba's primary international trading partner, its collapse sent shock waves across the island. Seemingly overnight, fertilizer, animal feed, herbicides, and textiles, as well as many parts for the country's few industries along with its Soviet-manufactured equipment, disappeared.

Cuba's economy went into a virtual free-fall. Its gross national production dropped over 30 percent in 1993 as compared to 1989. Sugar production hit a post-revolution single year low of 3.3 million tons annually, versus its high of 8.5 million tons. Electrical blackouts known as *apagónes* became more and more frequent. The Cuban government estimates that over 100,000 lost their jobs as an immediate result of the Soviet breakup. Outside observers believe that the real number is probably two to three times that amount.

With few imports and exports, the country's worst shortage became cash. Without outside currency, Cuba was destined to became not only an island in the Caribbean but also an island in the international economic sea. Now the Cuban peso had to be valued (or shall we say devalued) against the other currencies of the world. As of the first quarter of 2000, the U.S. dollar equaled roughly twenty Cuban pesos. It was all but impossible to maintain all aspects of socialism while being dragged into the world monetary system which is built on the cornerstone of capitalism. Both Cuba's peasant farmers and its economy returned to an era of the oxen and plow.

Cuba was forced to end many, once free, government services which in itself strikes at the core of socialism. Also instituted for the first time was a system of nationwide taxation. The money in circulation quickly dried up. The government began to reverse previous land nationalization laws and give back to the farmers idle land that had been nationalized for forty years. This was done in an effort to help increase the agricultural production of the country. By 1993, the land owned by the government dropped from 70 percent of the island to 33 percent.

To understand why the government owned almost three-quarters of the land in the country, you must go back to 1959. One of the most sweeping changes to the lives of the Cuban people after the revolution certainly was the Agrarian Reform law. Signed at La Plata in the Sierra Maestra Mountains on May 17, 1959, this nationalized all land owned by companies and foreign nationals. It also established the maximum land area an individual could own to 30 *caballerias*. This could be expanded to 100 *caballerias* if the farmer grew exportable crops like sugar cane or rice. This was a huge blow to the productivity of Cuba's agricultural-based economy. Simply put, everyone had less land to farm, therefore the production of the entire country dropped tremendously.

Less than five years later in October 1963, a second land reform law reduced the maximum land ownership by private individuals to only 5 *caballerias*. Even productive working farms above this size were nationalized. Most of this cultivated, producing land eventually returned to the tropical jungle from which it had once been claimed. The end result of this second reform was that 70 percent of the land was now under state ownership as national land. After this second post-revolution law, the government quickly promised that this would be the last land reform act to be instituted.

More recently the government took a step once viewed as incomprehensible in a socialist country—the authorization and encouragement of self-employment. By 1996 this foothold of capitalism had added over 200,000 jobs to the island nation's economy.

A Shortage of Everything Except Ingenuity

Out of necessity, the Cuban people have become very resourceful in almost every area of their lives. Nowhere is it more apparent than in their modes of transportation. Nothing goes to waste. Seldom does one person travel alone when two can share the same equipment. One problem is that transportation in the rural areas usually runs only until early to mid afternoon. If by that time you have not completed your trip and returned from where you have traveled, you will probably be forced to stay for the night. This puts a geographic limitation to the area traveled by most Cuban people.

Every evening, during our Cuban jaunt, we found ourselves on the road visiting yet another church. As our Volvo bus would approach a rural intersection, our headlights would pierce the Caribbean darkness to reveal dozens and sometimes hundreds of individuals running from their makeshift wait areas waving frantically in hopes of a ride. More than one of those waiting was destined to find themselves stranded for the night at the mercy of insects and the elements. Government vehicles, during the daytime, are obligated to pick up as many citizens as possible but this only puts a small dent in the transportation problem.

Remnants from Cuba's Russian connection: The infamous *Camel* is one of the few remaining buses in Cuba.

Hotels, motels and other overnight accommodations are virtually non-existent. Even if they did exist, most Cubans could not afford the price of a room. In fact, most Cuban peasants live and work very close to their homes. Many can live cradle to grave never traveling past fifty kilometers from their homes. A community church or a home chapel becomes even more important, for that which is located closest to them will have the greatest impact on their lives. International Cooperating Ministries (I.C.M.) has a plan to grid the island with churches every twenty-five kilometers. Each of these churches is then responsible for planting five more churches. The count, as of this writing, stands at 102 churches built by I.C.M. in just a few short years with forty-six under construction. ICM has 274 planned for the island gridding one every 12-1/2 square miles.

The Lowest Common Denominator

On any stretch of country road, you are more likely to witness half-a-dozen bicycles bearing down on you than a car or truck. The way the bicyclist is treated is indicative of the socialist doctrine. In socialism, all workers are treated equally. Whether you are a cashier, bus driver, or physician, you're treated the same. Driving down the road, all vehicles are treated the same also. It is not uncommon to find two bicyclists riding side by side near the right-hand side of the road. On more than one occasion, our forty-passenger bus would first slow down and then come to a crawl behind two bicycles, while waiting for bicycles coming from the opposite direction to clear the left-hand lane so that we could pass. No one gave this a second thought, neither the bicyclist nor the bus driver. I must say if I were on the bicycle and heard a forty-person Volvo bus downshifting, I would be inclined to leave the road. Even though Cuban law dictates that the bus must slow down, there is a more important law of physics at work in this situation. Still, forty years of socialism has taught bicyclists that they do not need to, nor will they,

This motorcycle with sidecar serves as a family vehicle for the pastor and the utility vehicle for an entire congregation.

move for a motorcycle, car, bus, or truck. This is an excellent example of how socialism slows everything and everyone, in some cases to a stop. It matters not whether we are talking about the speed of the vehicles, or productivity of the workers—everyone slows to the lowest common denominator. In this writer's humble opinion, there may be room for a philosophical discussion about the merits of socialism but, in practice, it simply does not work.

It is the rule rather than the exception that bicycles and motorcycles have an attached sidecar for passengers. Two, three or even more passengers can be seen sharing many sidecars. Commonly in the cities and countryside, enterprising young men with the word "taxi" stenciled on the seat back of their sidecar have begun their own capitalistic venture transporting passengers over short distances. This is one of the 150 plus government-permitted, self-employed activities now allowed in Cuba. Motorcycles outnumber cars three to one on the roads. It is truly amazing to see how many smiling Cuban children can be creatively stacked or hung from the sidecar of a motorcyclist. The record we saw for the weekend was seven. The father was driving the motorcycle with an eight-year-old girl in front of him, a fourteen-year-old boy on the rear holding tightly to his father's waist, while in the sidecar the mother carried three children, a two-year-old and four-year-old twins. Everyone looked happy as they headed to their destination as a family.

Ration Books

The government provides ration books for all workers. The Cubans' monthly ration is five pounds of rice, two pounds of beans, a pound of fish and eight eggs. Milk is reserved for babies and pregnant mothers. In addition to the monthly food ration, each person gets one pair of shoes and pants each year.

This means that a family will not starve, but these rations are barely enough to offer much more than basic life-sustaining meals. Still I marveled at how a family could make it on such meager food rations. You soon learn that in Cuba, life is based on survival rather than creature comforts.

We Are So Blessed

On our third day, with a hiss from its air brakes, our bus slowly came to a stop. Our group began to disembark at the building site of a small church located on a bluff overlooking miles of lush countryside. The footings had been dug and the walls had begun to rise skyward from the rocky Cuban soil. Our forty-foot bus coupled with seventeen disembarking Yankees turned out the entire community to inspect this most unusual spectacle. I had to wonder when they worked their jobs. In mid afternoon dozens of happy men, women and children milled about the building site. I began a conversation with one who spoke broken English. Broken or not, it was better than my non-existent Spanish. They told me that they live on their government rations coupled with what they could grow in the small gardens behind their homes. They then use most of their earned wages to help build the church. I think it was then that I felt the most ashamed. After all, I was almost fifty years old and this was my first attempt to share, above my normal tithe, some of what our family had been so blessed with. It made me want to cry. All I could think of was why had I been born in the richest country in the world and given so much and these people had so little. I do not know what God's complete plan for my life is but I do know that part of that plan must be for me to use some of what He has given to me to help build His kingdom, not only in my homeland, but also world-wide. I began to think as I stood on that building site, "I know that I can not do everything, but I am sure I could do something." If you have read this far in this book you know that you can help also. At this point I ask you to put this book down for a minute and ask God for His guidance with what He would have you do. Pray this simple prayer:

Father, I do not know all You have planned for my life. I do know I desire to serve You and to follow You. I desire to help fulfill the Great Commission You commanded. I pray for the wisdom to know what to do next. If You will give me this guidance I will follow Your will. I pray these things in the name of Jesus Christ.
Amen.

CHAPTER FIVE

The American Influence

The All-Mighty American Dollar

Cubans working in the cities and tourist areas get the added bonus of culling tips in the much-desired foreign currency. For many years the Cuban government resisted most forms of tourism. Today things have changed. Yearly, the country is now host to over two million visitors from around the world.

On our bus ride from the airplane to the customs checkpoint, I engaged in conversation with a jovial Canadian man whose graying hair was pulled into a foot-long ponytail. He reported, with great pride, that he has been spending six months a year in Cuba for the last fifteen years. Europeans are also making their way to the tropical island in increasing numbers. With the influx of foreign currency come also the many goods produced or resold outside of the United States and around the embargo. It is not abnormal when walking or driving down the street, to hear the latest sounds of *N-Sync* or the *Backstreet Boys* while some lucky girls show off eight-inch, thick-sole shoes or Calvin Klein jeans. Young boys can be seen sporting baggy pants slung so low it looks like gravity will take them the rest of the way down, just like those found hanging from the butts of kids in America.

It is estimated that, annually, just under one billion U.S. dollars flow into Cuba. Some comes from the tourist trade, others come from dollars sent or brought from visiting relatives. In a reversal from its earlier hard line on U.S. currency, the government itself now runs Dollar Stores. Many consumer goods not found anywhere else on the island can be purchased in these Dollar Stores, named because they only accept U.S. dollars as currency. The government-owned stores simply will not accept their own currency for purchases in these establishments.

Upsetting the Social Balance

This outside currency has, to some extent, upset the social balance in Cuba. In 1998 Fidel Castro was quoted as saying, "We used to live in a glass bowl, sanitary and pure, and now we're surrounded by viruses, bacteria, and egoism that the capitalist system creates." While that statement may be open to debate, the Cuban government will now do most anything for foreign currency, especially U.S. currency.

His Other Job

I met an athletic-looking Cuban physician, with graying temples and a warm smile, strolling past the Hotel Nacional. We made eye contact and he must have sensed I was not Cuban. He took a stab at a "Hello" in English to which I replied "Hello" in return. In Cuba it is still appropriate to simply greet a person on the street and introduce yourself, a feat not recommended on the streets of New York, Miami or Los Angeles. He spoke in very good English and welcomed me to Cuba. In our conversation he openly bragged of his "other job." He reported proudly that, in two days, he could earn more money selling trinkets at the

Morro Castle has guarded the entrance to the Port of Havana for decades

cruise ship docks, in downtown Havana near the Malecon, than he earned working at the Cuban hospital all month.

The Malecon

On the day we drove into old Havana, *Habana vieja,* our chosen route was the Malecon. This is the broad avenue that follows the curved coastline in the old downtown section for four miles. The Americans started the Malecon construction after the Spanish-American War just two years before the beginning of the twentieth century. If you use your imagination, the waves that crash on the sea wall, sending salt water twenty-feet high to now decaying stucco walls of the colonial row houses, can wash you to another time. At that time Havana was a destination for pleasure-seekers and the wealthy, and the three- and four-story row houses on the Malecon served as residences for the world's movers and shakers. Then, almost anything could be purchased in its upscale street-level shops. This was a time when beautiful women in expensive, sparkling evening gowns held the arms of dinner jacket-clad men as they made their way in through the cool evening breeze to places with names like the *Tropicana* and Papa Hemingway's favorite the *El Floridita*.

Today the glitter of the '40s and '50s is gone. All of its magnificence has now faded into crumbling crowded buildings, old cars and despair. The world's elite have moved to other places in the sun where they have to work much less at having fun.

The Malecon now leads past a breathtaking view of the Morro Castle, which has for decades guarded the entrance to the Port of Havana. This port leads to the docks, which bring the cruise ships with their passengers and, most importantly, their much desired and needed foreign currency to Havana.

The Brain Drain

To find where this problem originally began, you need to go back to 1959, just after the revolution, when more than 200,000 mainly upper- and middle-class Cubans began to flee the country. They took with them their wealth and, more importantly, their skills, knowledge and even their recipes, some handed down for generations. One example is the family of the famed Don Barcardi. Barcardi became a Cuban millionaire from the 1830s to the 1860s from his Barcardi Rum. In 1959 his family fled to Puerto Rico taking the family rum secrets with them. It is hard to calculate how much this one family has cost the Cuban economy. This exodus of the affluent has been referred to as Cuba's brain drain.

The "Brain Drain" that has resulted when over 500,000 of the countries brightest and wealthiest fled Castro from 1959 to today has done immeasurable damage

The years of 1965-1971 saw another 250,000 leave Cuba. In 1980 the Mariel boatlift witnessed another 125,000 coming to America's shores. This last flood of immigrants included an estimated 25,000 sent from Cuba's prisons.

From 1959 through 1989, the country was kept running financially mainly through Cuba's association with Moscow. The knockout blow to the Cuban economy came shortly after the Soviet Union began to fall apart in the early 1990s. Cuba's gross domestic product went into a free-fall of 35 percent in less than five years. The government countered this problem by finally legalizing the U.S. dollar in the early '90s, even though Cubans are still paid in Cuban pesos.

Creating a Limited-Market Economy

The government has allowed a limited-market economy to develop on the island. There are now over 150 permissible,

Children are the same everywhere

self-employed activities allowed by the government. The most desirable Cuban jobs are those which provide access to U.S. dollars. It is not uncommon at hotels and bars to find that your waiter or bartender may have been trained as a doctor, engineer or university professor. This toe-in-the-water stab at a market economy has helped the country economically struggle through, at best, a modest recovery.

Cubans can buy goods such as chicken, fruit, and vegetables in pesos. However, it is the government-owned Dollar Stores that offer luxury items such as sweets, canned hams, and consumer goods.

In fairness, some aspects of Cuban life can easily be viewed in a positive light. Most, who are knowledgeable, will agree that Cuba has one of the best education and health care systems available in any Third World country. On the negative side, constant and chronic shortages exist in everything from books to bandages to medicine. Both the present educational system and medical system were built post-revolution.

Cuba's Greatest Natural Resource— Its People

By far, the greatest of all the country's natural resources is its friendly and resourceful people. On the island there seems to be a shortage of everything, except ingenuity. Cuba is one of the most ethnically diverse islands in the Caribbean yet there are few clear-cut ethnic groups. The group which stands out, above all, is the Cuban children. Their angelic children cast a lasting impression, wherever you go. Beautiful children with dark eyes, warm smiles and ever-present laughter are not concerned with the future, but content to play and enjoy today in their sunny, Caribbean homeland. Primary school children can be seen in their maroon-colored uniforms while secondary school children sport uniforms of saffron. One cannot help but wonder what the next forty years will hold for them.

Castro the Hemisphere's Longest Leader

As of the year 2000, Fidel Castro will be seventy-four years old and has been in post-revolution power for over forty years. This is longer than any other world leader in our hemisphere. He is said to have an encyclopedic knowledge, ranging from engineering to cooking. Born on August 13, 1926, he graduated from prep school in 1945 where he was named best all-round athlete. That same year he entered the university to study law, earning his law degree in 1950.

In 1951, Fidel Castro made his first attempt at power, through the election process, by running for Cuba's congress. However, the elections were canceled because of a coup. Within eight years he would lead a band of revolutionaries to overthrow the Batista regime. One can only wonder what would have happened if the

Fidel Castro, now 74, has ruled with an iron hand since 1959 elections in 1951 had not been canceled. Though Castro rarely takes the podium for very long today, in his younger years he delivered very long speeches with fiery zeal. His record, without notes, is fourteen hours.

CHAPTER SIX

On the Road in Cuba

On the Road Again – Cuban Style

On Friday, April 7, we left Las Brisas Hotel in Playa Guardalauaca. With high hopes, we began our first day, in the eastern mountains of Cuba, visiting churches in the province of Holguín. This trip gave us a firsthand look at rural Cuban life.

The main road, which had more patches than smooth pavement, led from one of the nicest tourist areas in Eastern Cuba. The road would have been considered in dire need of repair in the poorest counties of the United States. Yet, it would prove to be one of the best roads we would travel during our trip. Each day our driver was on a continuous vigil, watching for a chicken, horse, cow, or goat, grazing unimpeded on the sides of the rural road, to wander into the roadway. Fences were all but nonexistent. As we passed hundreds of acres of sugarcane and banana trees, one couldn't help but see the economic damage done by forty years of socialism coupled with economic isolation. Many believe it is the economic sanctions alone that have caused the

Ernest (Che) Guevara, a young Argentinean physician who was a Commandant in the revolution, was killed while fighting with Bolivia rebels. Guevara has been idolized in death by the Cuban government.

problems in Cuba. While it is true that the sanctions have done long-term damage to the country, keep in mind that Cuba is free to trade worldwide with the exception of the United States. One must give some of the blame to a socialist society that gives no reward to those who strive to do more, while slowing the productivity of the masses to the level of the average.

Che Guevara—A Cuban Icon

The countryside is dotted with small block and frame homes in various stages of completion. Some appear to have been in the construction mode for years. These small homes line the road displaying a wide range of roofing materials from concrete to tin, and broken tiles to full thatched. A number of houses proudly display painted slogans saying, "Vía Fidel" and "Vía Che." The latter is a reference to Ernest (Che) Guevara, a young Argentinean physician who was a commandant in the revolution. In fact, there are more portraits of the deceased revolutionary leaders, like Che, than there are of Fidel on the island. Castro strongly discourages idolization of himself or any other living Cuban leader, but in death many are treated as martyrs no matter how their death occurred.

Che was killed in Bolivia several years after the Cuban revolution. He had left Cuba and was fighting with rebel forces there when he was killed by government troops. He has since become a national icon for Cuba. Today, we find his face, with his familiar patchy beard and low-slung beret, displayed on everything from books and posters to T-shirts and billboards.

Look What $5,000 Can Do!

Having successfully dodged the assorted roadside livestock, we found the first church we are to visit located in a quiet hillside community just outside of Holguín. The sign on the front of the church read "Monte de Salvacion" or the "Mountain of Salvation." We soon learned that this was a Pentecostal church. When we arrived, several members were on their knees praying with their faces buried in their Bibles, which were laid open on the simple wooden pews of the church.

To see what a budget of only $5,000 can do for a church in Cuba is beyond belief. I estimated that the parcel of land the church buildings were located on was over two acres. The complex included a home for the pastor, a church building for 150 members and two other buildings. The cost to purchase the land to build the church divided by the number of members is less than forty dollars per member. For less than what most

For only a $5,000 budget, over two acres of land was purchased in Holguin, and this church and the pastor's home was built

American couples pay for an evening meal, the I.C.M. ministry can give a church home to the Christians and seekers of this community. Considering the members in this church now and in the future, and the five churches they are to plant, hundreds will have the opportunity to receive eternal salvation through this church ministry. Quite a bargain, I'm sure you will agree.

We can sometimes lose sight of the fact that these are real people. Each one who hears the gospel is someone's brother, sister, mother or dad. If you look at the I.C.M. ministry in this light, with the faces of your family replacing faceless Cubans you have never met, I am sure you would agree that forty dollars each for the chance to receive eternal life in heaven is worth every penny.

The pastor introduced us to his wife and three beautiful daughters ranging in age from fifteen to nineteen. Through our interpreter, we learned that the oldest daughter was turning nineteen that day. Our group joined together in a rousing round of "Happy Birthday." Her father then added that she was still single and looking for a husband. This produced a blush to her cheeks that could be seen from across the building.

After a tour of the church, a prayer and well-wishes from all, we headed east to the waterfront community of Antilla located on the northeast side of the island.

Off Again

As our bus rolled into the seaside village of Antilla, also located in the province of Holguín, we became the center of attention. We slowly made our way down the narrow streets to the church and, on our way, we passed a park in the center of town. Several hundred adults were sitting under the trees, patiently waiting. We were told that they were waiting for their weekly ration of food vouchers. Our guide said that these waits can range from a few hours to days. Thousands of man-hours of productivity are wasted everywhere we looked. Cubans are taught early to patiently wait—wait for food vouchers, wait to turn in the vouchers for food, wait for a ride. Waiting is a way of life in Cuba.

Take a Number Please

The Cuban people that we met across the island seemed unaffected by waiting. Through generations, they have come to expect it as a normal part of life. I would venture a guess that few Cubans are afflicted with stress-related diseases.

As our trip continued we passed a cock-fighting arena and a number of old five-story tenement buildings looking like large, filthy concrete boxes. Most of these apartments had laundry drying in the cool sea breeze, which resembled the flying flags of an ancient Naval Armada.

Public Transportation— Or the Lack Thereof

For several minutes our bus slowed to a virtual crawl while following one of the hundreds of horse-drawn carts we had seen. This one was carrying a load of green bananas piled much higher than seemed safe or even possible. As we finally passed we saw enough children hanging on the front of the cart to field a good soccer team. Our slow pace while waiting to pass allowed us to view two great examples of Cuban public transportation as they caught up with our bus from the rear.

The first was a 1945 Ford truck with a converted cattle trailer attached to its bed. This trailer had portholes roughly cut into the metal sides. The portholes covered the sides and rear, allowing people of all ages to protrude from their chest up, as the truck slowly made its way down the road. The second vehicle was a flatbed truck with wooden slats on the sides to keep people from falling during its slow swaying forward movement. As the vehicle lumbered down the road, thirty to fifty people held each other up as they slowly swayed from side to side in unison. As this vehicle passed an intersection, a number of people advanced to the road with a hand held high hoping to catch a ride, but both vehicles were filled to, and, one might argue, beyond capacity.

A Permit is Needed for Everything

Upon arrival at the church in Antilla, the pastor, an engineer by education, met us. He is married to a doctor who is expecting their first child. He gave up his government job to serve the Lord full-time. His wife, who was due in only two months, had applied to move to a medical facility closer to home. We were

Our family's second project in Cuba: Antilla in the province of Holguin

told that her application is still pending. When asked how long they felt it will be, her reply was simply two hands lifted upwards and a smile. Concerning this application, as with most things in Cuba, the order of the day is to simply wait, with no idea how long it will take to hear the disposition of the request. I can hardly wait for the next time I hear an employee in the United States complaining about their job to relate the story of this pastor's wife.

The church building displayed proudly—near the top—a concrete etching establishing 1913 as the date the building was built. An additional plaque by the front door showed that the last renovation of the building took place in 1958, over forty years ago. The two-story building is the worship hall for over 250 members, although the seating will barely handle a hundred. Four major services are held in this church weekly. The $5,000 budget on this church provided a newly poured concrete floor to replace the old wooden floor. We are told that the wooden floor was in such bad shape that one Sunday a member, while walking across the church, fell through the floor itself.

Location, Location, Location

Just to the south, the church had a vacant lot approximately thirty feet wide. During the conversation with the church leaders, we also found out that the house immediately to the south of the vacant lot could be purchased for $1,500. A tour of the adjoining property showed a shotgun-type layout with three small bedrooms off a long, dark narrow hallway leading to a makeshift kitchen and bathroom. The outside walls of the house stopped two feet short of the eaves. I saw a bird fly through the space into the kitchen and then back out again. The owner showed no concern for the bird as she continued her tour with sweeping hand gestures and a large toothless smile. While the house may not be much from our standards, it had the three most important components for any good real estate purchase: Location, Location, Location! In our case it was located next to our church.

After a quick powwow with my son, Shane, we agreed it felt right to claim this church as the first project to be funded from Joshua's newly formed foundation. Josh was Shane's son and my grandson. He was a two-and-a-half-year-old, redheaded boy with bright eyes, a cheery disposition, and the wide-eyed inquisitiveness of any small child. One thing for certain, Josh was all boy. He loved to push buttons—buttons on the microwave, buttons on the television, buttons in the car. Josh certainly knew how to push the buttons in our heart.

CHAPTER SEVEN

Joshua Bryce Cole
1995-1998

A Gift from God

Josh came into this world on a clear September day in 1995. His stay with us was brief; for only two and a half short years we had the wonderful pleasure of raising and loving this gift from God. Early on Monday morning, February 16, 1998, Joshua was taken from us when he died in his sleep. When he went to bed the night before, the most important thing on his mind was whether he got another bottle at bedtime. Silently and with no apparent cause, he was taken by death early in the morning. This was the hardest mountain my family and I have ever been forced to climb. Why did this happen? How could he have been taken at such a young age? Why, with no cause of death, was he not here to enjoy his life?

I will never forget the morning that the Melbourne Beach policeman came to our front door to tell us the grim news of Josh's death. My wife and I both felt numb as we quickly dressed ourselves for the short one-mile ride, in our little beachfront community, to our son Shane's home. Entering his home, I saw Shane sitting on the couch with his head in his hands sobbing uncontrollably. Already gathered at his home were neighbors, family, police, and paramedics. Josh's little body, still in his diapers, lay quietly in his bedroom. The rest of the family came together in my son's time of need.

Our Friends Come to Our Family's Side

What can anyone say that will give you comfort at a time like this? What can anyone do to ease your pain? I can assure you there are no words that can be spoken at a time like that which will make any difference at all. All I could do was embrace my son, hold his head close to my chest and rub his back with fatherly love as he and I continued to cry. In the next several days, all the normal questions would be asked. Why us? Why Josh? Why now? Why so young?

I never knew how many true friends we had across this country until the loss of my grandson. Our family received hundreds of cards and letters from friends scattered from Washington State to New York, from California to Florida. For years I have trained Financial Services professionals across this great country. Now it was these friends who came to give back to my family and me. I had mentioned, almost as an afterthought, that I did not want flowers sent to Josh's funeral. To me, it seemed a waste of flowers and the money spent to purchase them just to have them bake quickly in the Florida sun clustered around the final resting place of little Josh's earthly body. Personally, the grave meant little to me. I knew that Josh was not buried in that Florida sand, but instead he was enjoying eternal life in heaven with our Lord and Savior, Jesus Christ. I also knew that I would see him again one day. However, as the head of the family, my wife Joan and I solemnly walked through the steps required to bring closure to the earthly body of our young grandson. Picking out caskets barely three feet long is a task that I would wish on no one. Somehow we got through that painful ordeal.

The Unexpected Money

Quite unexpectedly, within the next few days, checks began arriving, enclosed in the hundreds of cards and letters received from friends, family, and coworkers. Somehow my request for no flowers had been translated instead into sending donations. I am sure that the donors thought their gifts would ultimately go to a group which researched whatever medical condition Josh's death was determined to have been caused by. Was it Sudden Infant Death Syndrome (SIDS)? Was it a congenital heart problem? We simply did not know. Through the eight weeks it took to get the final autopsy report, the cards, letters, books, Bible verses, book markers, condolences and checks continued to arrive.

At the end of the autopsy process, the medical examiner announced that they had found no cause for Josh's death. I did not realize, until that time, that an autopsy performed on a young child does not begin by seeking the cause of death, but rather by systematically eliminating what did not cause the death. They begin with the obvious. Are there bruises, broken bones, or signs of trauma? From there they go through toxicology screenings, search for congenital problems, diseases, or any other clue that could solve this horrible mystery. In the end, everything was negative. Simply put, Josh should still be alive—only he was not. You always assume your children and grand-children will outlive you. There is something unnatural about burying a child or grandchild.

Slowly Putting our Lives Back Together

As we slowly began to resume our lives, little by little, day by day, I turned to the only place I knew to find the strength to move past this horrible tragedy. I went to my knees and there I found the strength to move forward.

Why is it that bad things happen to good people? The truth of the matter is bad things happen to good people and to bad people. Bad things just simply happen to people. Part of life is being born and part of life is dying. God does not give each of us equal portions of talent, ability, or even time on this earth. I believe strongly that we are all judged more for the direction we take than the distance we cover during our short stay on this spinning rock called "Earth." In the scheme of an eternity, our life here is but a fleeting moment. While we miss Josh, I would bet where he is now, he does not miss this earth. Him there, and us here, both have assurance from our Lord and Savior, Jesus Christ that we will, one day, be together again.

The Josh Cole Foundation

Now we as a family were left with a decision: what to do with all the checks made payable to the Josh Cole Fund. Without a cause of death, there was no organization that seemed to be the logical recipient of the funds. The one thing our family agreed on is that we wanted these funds to make a difference. It took us a while but eventually we completed the steps necessary to place these funds into a family foundation. The name of the foundation is the Josh Cole Foundation. The funds we received from our friends and loved ones became the initial deposit in this foundation. Our family agreed that each year we would

continue to contribute to this foundation. The only require-
ment we would place on the funds use is that in some way, the
money would be used to benefit the life of a child or children.

Josh Touches His First Children

The first of our distributions was used to help a father, in our
county, who lost his wife during the delivery of twins. A young
boy, in his early twemties, had a two-year-old son and now twin
newborns to take care of with only a meager manual-labor
income. A story in our local paper brought him to our attention.
We took some pleasure in knowing that because Josh had lived,
there were funds available to help the father stay home with the
newborns for the first few weeks of their life.

The next distribution was to buy generators and supplies
for a family in Puerto Rico, after a killer hurricane sideswiped
the island. A young man who worked with my son, Shane, had
family on that island who had lost everything in the storm.
Shane brought the need to our family. We quickly agreed that
the children in this Puerto Rican family could greatly benefit
from some funds from Josh's foundation.

Because Josh Lived

Now we found ourselves standing in Cuba outside a church in
bad need of repair and expansion, too small to handle the needs
of the 250-plus members, a full one-third of them children.
What better use of these funds could there be than to give a
church building that will affect so positively the lives of mothers, fathers and children alike.

The existing church seats just over one hundred. The pastor
told us that on Sundays the overflow crowd stands outside in the
hot tropical sun to hear the word of God. There is no room for
a Sunday school class to teach the children of the love of Jesus.
We are told that the house next door is for sale. The asking price
was $1,500. It should take only another $500 to do the needed

renovations. Yes, you read those numbers correctly. Less than two thousand dollars would buy and renovate the building.

Shane and I agreed this was a fitting tribute to that flaming redheaded boy that we all loved so much.

We, as a family, funded the first church in Havana, in memory of Josh. Shane and I would visit that church in just two days to present a picture of our little guy. However, this church would be the first to use the funds from Josh's foundation. Once this church's expansion and renovation is completed, the pastor tells us that the morning worship service could easily swell from 250 to 500 worshipers. I think Joshua would be pleased.

You Too Can Make a Difference

I would like to encourage you to think of making one of the churches in Cuba a fitting tribute to a saintly mother, father or loved one. Maybe it is the person who led you to the Lord. I could not think of a more fitting tribute. Just indicate your desire to help on the "Yes I Want to Help" page at the end of this book and send it to us. We will be glad to talk to you personally to discuss the steps involved in building a church in Cuba. Maybe you would like to go to Cuba with us to see firsthand what a difference your gift can make. If you do not feel led to build a church but would like to make a one-time gift or a monthly donation just indicate that on the "Yes I Want to Help" page or visit our web site at www.CubaStory.com I know the Lord will bless you for it.

Eleven Thousand Divided by Five

In Antilla, a city of eleven thousand with only five churches, we believe the goals of this small Methodist church are more than realistic. My son and I rejoice with thoughts of how many will find salvation in our Lord and Savior, Jesus Christ through this church. I know Josh is smiling in heaven. This will only add to the joy of our family's reunion as we one day are united in heaven.

CHAPTER EIGHT

When Bad Things Happen to Good People

Reverend Chuck's Bible Study

A fine man of God, Rev. Chuck Magruder wrote a Bible study lesson in 1997 on God's love through tragedy. While writing this book I came across his scripture lesson from 1 Peter 5:1-11. It touched me and gave even more insight into God's love and how hard it is to accept that bad things can happen to good people.

He told the story of Laura Carter, a freshman at Dennison University in Granville, Ohio. On Parents' Weekend she, her parents, and three friends drove into Columbus. Driving on East Broad St. they heard what sounded like a car backfiring. Laura, riding in the back seat, slumped forward. An hour later she was pronounced dead from a single gunshot wound to the chest. The police investigation revealed an incredible sequence of events.

Shortly before the Carter car arrived at the intersection, another car almost two blocks away had caused property damage by making a U-turn. Witnesses said a man jumped from the car which caused the damage while three others began shooting at him. One of those bullets, fired from over a block away entered the Carter car at the precise moment that it crossed the intersection causing the death of the bright young eighteen-year-old coed.

I can certainly relate to the anguish felt by that family having traveled much the same road when we lost little Josh. Hopefully nothing quite so dramatic or terrible has happened to you. But, all of us have had difficult times in our lives. During these tough times we may wonder, "Does God really love me?" Sometimes we can even doubt the text in verse 7: "Cast all your care on him, for he cares for you." We have all thought, "If God does love us why do the innocent and righteous have to suffer?" How can we keep our faith during these times? To keep our faith strong we should focus on three principles.

1. God is Not the Author of Evil

We know in our hearts that God does not create evil. But, how many times do we hear people blame God when things go wrong? "Why did God let this happen to me," we hear them say. It is a weakness that can be found even in spiritual giants such as Billy Graham. In his autobiography, *Just As I Am*, he tells a story of how, in 1954, he had the opportunity to preach in the same stadium where Hitler had spoken. He was suddenly hit with excruciating pain from a kidney stone. This great man of God was heard as he cried out, "Why is God doing this to me?" We have all been there and thought these thoughts. It is easy to give praise to God when things in our life are running smoothly. But during financial problems, health problems or death of a loved one, we think it is suddenly His fault.

You only have to go back to the challenges Job faced to see true suffering. Job was a man of wealth who lost it all. A man with ten beautiful children, he prayed for them daily and he lost them all. He was strong and healthy and became painfully afflicted. If ever anyone had the reason to cry out, "Why have You let this happen to me, God?" it was Job. But, he would not.

We should also remember the words of James 1:13: "When tempted, no one should say, God is tempting me for God cannot be tempted with evil nor does He tempt anyone."

Remember there are forces alive and active in the world other than God. There are forces of nature that may bring disaster and suffering. There are complex processes in our bodies and in society that bring suffering upon us. We should remember that much of our suffering is due to our own unwise choices and planning. Then, too, there is chance. A combination of two or more events, unplanned, unforeseen and undesired, causes what we refer to as an accident. For example, the car that carried Laura Carter through that intersection at the precise moment a stray bullet arrived to kill her. There are also the forces of evil that cannot be overlooked. This evil is Satan himself. Satan is as real as God. You cannot believe that the Bible is the word of God without believing that, as stated in the, Bible there is a Satan.

What does this realization that there are forces other than God at work in the world do for you? It will free you from the false idea that God is to blame for all the difficulties that come upon you. Once you are freed you can see God does care for you. Then you can believe in God's love for you in spite of your circumstances.

2. God Can Turn Circumstances into Victories

These victories can be accomplished if we position ourselves through faith to allow Him to turn our tragedies into His victories. Look at Job. He came through his trials like purified gold. God blessed the latter part of his life more than the first. Our tragedies can be useful, because they can be the reason for keeping us dependent upon God.

To see the ultimate victory over tragedy, just look at the cross. The darkest hour in all of history was when Jesus died upon the cross. It looked like defeat of everything God was trying to do in His Son. But, wait! Keep faith in the God who turns circumstances into victory. Christ died, was buried and then was raised from the dead. The resurrection is God's greatest victory but could not have happened unless Christ had first died. Surely if God could turn the cross into victory, He could turn your problems into something positive also. I see now, that every day, God is having more and more of an impact on my life and the lives of others because of the untimely death of my grandson.

Think about this! What if God's care for us is seen after, rather than before the misfortune or trial? What if God takes care of us by reshaping us rather than protecting us from our trials? Remember, the life you are living now is not the only one possible for you. You are capable of infinite change and redirection in your life. God is always working to bring that about. In Romans 8:28, we read: "We know that in all things God works for the good of those who have been called according to His purpose." The next verse plainly tells us that His purpose is to use all the circumstances of our life to make us more like Jesus.

The point is simple. You may not be altogether responsible for what comes into your life, but you are responsible for how you react to it. While circumstances may tend to lead us one way, if we look closely, we can see that God cares for us as He always has. And if we will only allow Him, He can bring victory out of our pain no matter how difficult that pain is.

3. God's Ultimate Goal Transcends This Life.

Lift your eyes beyond today's horizon. Far too often we look upon adversity and misfortune as if this life is all that counts. After all, how long does human life last? Sixty, seventy or maybe even one hundred years? No life goes on forever!

What will this belief do for you when a terminal disease or a fatal accident strikes you or a loved one? Do you give up faith in God caring for you? No! Remember the twenty-third psalm:

"The Lord is my shepherd, I shall not want." He knows what is best for each of us. So, God's love and care for us is seen in this life, at the moment of death, through death, and on the other side of death. How long then does God care for you? Forever! Literally, forever!

In the last analysis, however, as you face your own personal disaster and are tempted to become angry toward God, you must make your own peace.

In the end understand that God cares for you. How you react to this simple and basic truth is up to you. While your struggle may be intensely personal, you must keep the right perspective on problems when they come. And they will come—sooner or later. That's part of life.

CHAPTER NINE

Cuba's Revival

Our Second Birthday of the Day

The third stop of that first day was to an Assembly of God church in Cacocan. Well into the construction process, this solid concrete church was having a coat of stucco applied to the interior walls when we arrived. The pastor, his wife, their two beautiful little girls along with a dozen members of the congregation welcomed us. All were busy working on the construction of their new house of worship. Today, ironically, was the pastor's birthday, our second birthday for the day. Everyone shared pats on the back and hugs in Christian love as another rousing round of "Happy Birthday" was sung.

We were there we all clustered around the pastor, laying hands on him and praying for his church. I must say, even though it was the pastor's birthday, we left with the gift.

Revival Sweeping the Island

Before we left, he told us the story of how revival is sweeping this small island nation. He said in homes, churches, lean-tos

The top photo show where the Assembly of God Church in Cacocan is currently meeting. The building shown on the bottom right is where th 150+ member church will call home. Total budget is $5,000 for the land and building.

and garages all across the nation, Cubans are coming to Christ by the thousands. I ponder the future by looking at the past. One of the areas that all socialist governments focus their attention on is the youth. An area the Cuban government takes the greatest pride in is the country's educational system. In primary and secondary educational systems they teach the children the virtues of socialism.

In essence, they understand that to teach a child is to plant the seed that can change the world. How can an entire country enthralled in forty years of socialization be changed? It is by changing the hearts and minds of the people. When you become a Christian, you become a member of the Fellowship of Christ.

You share something greater than any government or ideological principle. These new Christians are also like children. They are new children in Christ. Their minds and hearts are not unlike that of a child, ready to be shaped and molded.

How to Change a Country

Admittedly, I am not an expert in what trends it takes to change a country or a culture. However, I do strongly feel the best step one can take in affecting positive change is to expand Christianity in a nation, much the same way it is now spreading across Cuba.

We boarded the bus, praising God for allowing us to partner with churches like these and for the opportunity to play a small part in His great plan. It is to Him that we give the glory for this trip and this ministry.

What Was Expected—Not This

Our next stop was a quick one that allowed us to view a prospective lot on which to build a new church. Then we were off for an hour-and-a-half drive through the countryside to a small hamlet called Ohama for the dedication of a new church building. This was destined to become the highlight of our first day in Cuba. We knew that there was a dedication service planned, but none of us had any idea what lay in store for us only a few kilometers up a winding, royal-palm-lined country road.

Like Moses Parting the Red Sea

Our bus slowly lumbered down a narrow dirt road with shallow ditches on each side. Beside the road are tiny, dimly-lit homes of the village. I can assure you that I would never have driven a passenger car down this road, but that did not prevent our fearless bus driver from pressing forward. Our headlights pierced the tropical darkness and slowly we could begin to make out a small group of people in the road ahead. "This must be the place," our leader, Dois Rosser, announced. He, along with the

In Omaha, over 600 turn out for the dedication service, with half the attendees worshiping outside. The building was just completed and it already needs to double its size. Total cost for land and building, under $8,000

rest of us had never been to this facility. I could not help but think that we were traveling down this road much like we came to Cuba, by faith. As we drew closer, the small crowd began to grow, and then a cheer began to crescendo through the Cuban night. As we rolled to a stop, the headlights of the bus shone on over two hundred smiling faces waiting to greet us.

They began to clap in unison and sing. The door to our bus opened and a cheer from the crowd, befitting any returning college football team after winning a national title, rang out. Anyone can tell the difference between an obligatory welcome and a group that is truly glad to see you. This group was truly glad to see us. In single file, we began to step off the bus. Like Moses parting the Red Sea, the crowd separated and the mass of humanity formed a pathway to the little pink and white stucco building.

The cross of Calvary, the symbol of our Christian faith, hung above the door. People reached to touch and graciously pat us on the back as we, one by one, walked through a gauntlet of smiling well wishers. In broken English, the phrases that were repeated the most were "God bless you" and "Thank you." I do not know what I expected, but it certainly was not this.

A Fire Marshal's Worst Nightmare

As we entered the church, the 200-person greeting party in front of the church was replaced by over 150, seated on every inch of the pews inside, with the exception of seventeen seats reserved for us, as a place of honor, in the first two rows. Forty years of political strife between Cuba and the United States seemed to have never existed on that starry, warm night in Ohama.

Within a few minutes, a young man struck a single chord on a cheap, plastic, electric piano and on cue the crowd began to rock. The most straight-laced traditionalist would not have been able to keep their foot from tapping to the Latin-Salsa beat as it began to ring through this house of worship. With hands clapping and hips swaying, eyes turned towards heaven, the church congregation began to praise Jesus Christ, the only Son of the only living God. You could feel the Holy Spirit in that room. Then the elders of the church began bringing those worshipers, who had welcomed us, into the building.

Much like civilians would begin an impromptu direction of traffic at a roadside accident, with arms waving and hands pointing, they guided the members in through the back door. One by one they entered in, filling every square inch of floor on both sides of the pews. Then came the children. Children, children and more children poured in until somewhere between seventy-five and one hundred sat between the first row of pews and the foot of the altar. Lastly, a solid tide of humanity began a slow march down the main aisle, four and five wide, until they filled the remaining space leading up to the children's area. The whole time the pounding salsa beat kept the crowd going. It took a moment for me to step to the front of the church, turn around and take a picture. Not another person could have made it into that building. This was a fire marshal's worst nightmare.

Buildings Reach People – Building Involves People

Even with darkness cloaking the church building, it was easy to see how happy and thankful this church was to have a home. Growing up in churches in America, I have heard a cliché repeated in churches time and time again, "Buildings do not matter…people do." While I agree that a man's soul is much more important than the church buildings, these churches in Cuba are a very important component to the evangelizing of that country.

As we made the trip to the church earlier that night, we were met by one of the main Protestant leaders of the island, just a few miles from the church. He stepped on our bus with his wife and, through our interpreter, told us that the church had been preparing for this day for months. A group of ladies had been scrubbing the floor all day to make a positive impression on us. He told of dozens of women on their hands and knees with buckets scrubbing every inch of the floor of the church. It was only then, sitting on the front row, that I noticed for the first time that the floor had the dull gray appearance of brushed concrete. There was neither tile nor carpet but, I assure you, it was clean enough to eat from.

The Latin-Salsa Music Reaches the People

There, in the front of the church, was the praise band: a drummer, electric piano, and several singers all producing a Latin sound that made it exciting to be in the room. I would later be told, by one of the island's religious leaders, that for years the Protestant movement had tried to reach the people with more traditional music and worship services. This failed to produce anywhere close to the result now sweeping the island.

As he explained it, this driving Latin beat can be found in most of the island music. Then why not church? Once the church music was made more appealing, the attendance began to increase. This music could be heard at every stop we made. Whether in Havana or the rural cities in the Sierra Maestra Mountains, not once did I hear a slow ballad. Always it was the upbeat Latin sound and the foot-tapping praise music that was found in all of the worship services.

By the luck of the draw, I was in the front row only a few feet from the platform. From that vantage point, I had an excellent view of the musicians as well as the opportunity to observe, at close range, their musical equipment.

Meager Equipment but a Big Sound

The electric piano came out of its original, but very worn, cardboard packaging complete with the molded styrofoam pieces used in shipping. Two of the members began unpacking the piano very carefully. You would have thought that this box contained the Holy Grail itself.

Additionally, the congregation was the proud owner of three different microphones, none with a microphone stand. They were passed between the musicians and the pastors with an efficiency that could only be achieved through practice. During one solo sung by the pianist, one of her fellow musicians became a human microphone stand by holding the microphone a few inches from her mouth while she fingered out the chords to a praise song.

The amplifiers looked like they had been salvaged from an electronic junkyard—not one knob remained on either of the two units. Cables were consistently jiggled to produce the proper connection that would ultimately emit the sound. Once these wires were arranged properly, however, the two small amps did their job. The house was jumping!

Our Congo Line Exit Reveals Even More

For the next hour, a nonstop succession of dancers, children's choirs, and pastors praised God and entertained the crowd. Before I knew it an hour and a half had passed. Since we had a long trip back to the hotel, our group was forced to bid a fond farewell to the church. We were led Congo-line style across the front platform which allowed us to exit a rear door while the music blared, hands clapped and voices pierced the dark Cuban night.

As I left the building I felt the cool ocean breeze of the night. I walked around the outside of the building and turned back toward the front of the building where our bus sat waiting. It was only then that I received the full impact of the night. Not only was every square inch of that church filled with believers, but standing three- to five-people deep in a U-shape around both sides and the front of the building was another two to three hundred worshipers. They were all huddled closely to the outside walls of the building as they peered through the burglar-bar ironwork that covered the windows.

Once we had all returned to the bus, a conversation ensued trying to estimate the number of attendees. The consensus was that somewhere between 600 and 650 worshipers had been at the dedication of a church built to seat 150.

This church, which by our standards seems crude—with its concrete floor, pink, white, and green walls, no air conditioning, wall-mounted oscillating fans to stir the humid air, and two small twelve-inch amplifiers used for a PA system—was God's house. That night He was there. And, praise be to Him, so were we.

That Bed Sure Looks Good

It was after 11:00 P.M. when we arrived at the Kohly Hotel, still wired on the natural high created by the excitement and spirit of God. After replaying the day's events over and over in my mind, I finally drifted into a tentative slumber. A few hours later I was abruptly jerked back to consciousness by an abnormally, loud phone delivering my 5:00 A.M. wake-up call in the universal language of rapid, loud rings. Shane and I dressed and left for the dining room.

CHAPTER TEN

Our Second Day

A Stately Old Building

By the light of day, I developed a better appreciation for our older, but well-maintained, hotel. There was no doubt that this hotel was one that was designated for the foreign tourist, who bring the much-needed currency to the island.

Even before 6:00 A.M., there were two hotel maids mopping the long ceramic-tile hallways on each of the five floors. The sun was shining through an open window at the east end of the building, and the section of the floor which had not yet been painstakingly mopped, still sparkled. The thick mahogany doors to the sleeping rooms matched the mahogany baseboards and chair rail, which ran the length of the long hallway. This beautiful woodwork was obviously handcrafted by Cuban carpenters who took great pride in their work.

We passed through the bright, breezy lobby so typical of Caribbean hotels. It was surrounded with every type of tropical

Cuba turns to tourism in search of hard currency. In the process, they create a tourist aparthied. Shane looks out our balcony at the pool area of the Kohly Hotel

plant imaginable. I paused for a moment to watch a humming-bird; or "Doctor Bird" as they are called in the Caribbean, as it flitted from one bougainvillea plant to another. Around the pool I noticed what must be a half acre of bird of paradise plants. I was impressed by how beautiful and well-manicured the grounds were.

You Don't Get This with a Ration Card

Upon entering the dining room we were shown to our seats. Most hotel rates for tourists are all-inclusive and boast fabulous buffets. I was reminded, as I walked through the forty-foot buffet line, of the ration cards which sustain most Cubans. I suddenly did not know if I should be feeling grateful or ashamed.

After breakfast and two cups of Cuban coffee that was strong enough to stand a spoon on its end, we were ready to begin our four-hour trip southeast to Guantánamo. This is the same province which houses the more than one hundred-year-old United States Naval base on the southeastern section of the island.

On to Getmo

The province of Guantánamo faces both Haiti and Jamaica. The long ride gave some of our group the opportunity to know each other better while some simply tried to get caught up on their sleep. Once we entered the city of Guantánamo, we began to wind through its tight streets. As we paused to make a sharp turn down what appeared to be a side street, we heard the sounds of singing. One block later we pulled curbside to the church. Unlike the other small churches and home chapels we had seen so far, this one was the largest church building yet—two stories with a red tin roof and a fresh stucco exterior. The beautiful wood-framed windows were in the traditional arch shape you would expect to see in churches all across the world. Inside, more than 500 worshipers were lifting their hands, hearts and voices to Jesus.

Entering the building we walked across rich-looking black tile as we made our way to the reserved seats in the front of the church. Again the church was packed to capacity. Looking over my shoulder, I see two balconies also packed. Behind the altar was a backdrop of flat river rock mounted on the wall in a huge arch shape towering over fifteen feet high. Embedded in the center of the flat rock was a cross, which was illuminated from behind. This building in any other community, would be considered a very nice facility and would not seem out of place in our own Florida cities.

By now, it was 10:30 on Saturday morning. There were over 500 people swaying to the Latin-salsa beat of a ten piece praise band with guitars, electric piano, saxophone, clarinet and, of course, the ever-present drum set and Congos. Later that day we learned that the service had been going for an hour before we arrived.

The Three Hour Song Service

For the next two hours we sang. No praying, no preaching, just singing. On our feet, hands held high, that pounding beat had drawn a crowd to the streets of downtown Guantánamo. Men, women, and children sang at the top of their lungs. The presence of the Holy Spirit could be felt in this church the moment we stopped curbside.

The 360 Bounce

The majority of the children and many of the adults also danced while they sang. Many simply bounced up and down in place while occasionally turning 360 degrees. It was contagious. I had to give the 360 degree bounce at least one try. I must admit it was uplifting. I also produced quite a bit of laughter as several children, who covered their mouths, squatted and pointed in laughter as my 250-pound body left the ground repetitively.

The Rocking Chair Brigade

To the left of the altar was a group of six wooden rocking chairs reserved for the mothers with six-month to eighteen-month old babies. This section was filled to capacity. In fact, I would estimate that a full one-third of the congregation was under the age of fifteen. The churches in Cuba are reaching the children.

Children are Children Everywhere

With little to do and few diversions, the church becomes a strong part of the community and draws children from many families, even some where adults refuse to participate. Christ during his ministry on earth said, in Matthew 19:14: "Let the little children come to Me, and do not hinder them, for the kingdom of heaven belongs to such as these." Smiles on the faces of these children are something to behold. We have all seen children at church or other events whose facial and body language says, "I'm so bored," or, "I

(Top) The children present a dance recital in our honor at the Guantanamo Bay church. (Center) The building is magnificent by Cuban standards. (Bottom) The Praise Band energizes the crowd with a Latin Salsa Beat.

want to leave; this is not cool." No such look can be found on the faces of the children in this church.

As we worshiped, one of my fellow I.C.M. travelers leaned over to me and asked the question, "How many do you think you could get at your church on Saturday morning?" I did not bother to reply. His point was well taken.

Two Special Gifts Exchanged in Song

At 12:30 we finished the song portion of the service and took our seats for the message. By 1:30 the pastor had finished and it was back to the singing again. A quartet of four young ladies named "God as Heard" began to sing. We noticed that they were actually singing in English and later found out not one of them spoke English. However, they had worked for over a month to learn the words of the song "I Am Free" in English as a tribute to us. It was a wonderful gesture that was made even better when we learned of the amount of work put into the project.

As the pastor introduced each member of our group, we took our place on the stage. Our leader, Dois Rosser, reported to the congregation that in return for the hard work the four young ladies had put into learning the song in English, we also were prepared to sing a song to them in Spanish. There was silence as they listened, ready to hear what song we chose. The title of the song was "Hallelujah." The word *hallelujah* was also the only word in the song. As we began to sing, the entire congregation came alive. Clapping their hands they joined in song with us. Most of us on stage were surprised, but quickly learned that the word *hallelujah* is the same in both English and Spanish. So we cheated a little bit. The congregation loved it. We did too; it felt great to be part of a group of five hundred Christian brothers and sisters joined together in a bilingual praise to God.

They Wanted to Be There

By this time fifty to seventy-five children, under the age of ten, gathered in front of the altar doing their in-place 360 degree jumps. Amazingly, after four hours in church, their smiles were still intact. These kids were not putting on an act. You could tell that each of them wanted to be there, on Saturday morning, in the house of the Lord, praising Him. At one point, an eighteen-month old boy, swaying his hips while his mother held on to him, suddenly stopped. The mother instinctively placed him on the floor. He squatted and began to produce a puddle at his mother's feet. In a flash, one of the deacons appeared with a mop and cleaned up the puddle as the mother changed the tiny dancer. Once both the deacon's and the mother's job was finished, everyone went back to the vertical 360 degree hop.

Witnessing to the Government Official

The quality craftsmanship of the church's woodwork was beautiful and done entirely by the members. A department in the Cuban government works to preserve the historic properties of the island. We later learned that the head of the department personally visited this church in Getmo (local jargon for Guantánamo) after its completion and asked, "How did you do such a good job?" The pastor replied, "We had to do our best work; this place was built to glorify Jesus Christ." Not only did they finish a beautiful church but also had an opportunity to witness, to one government official, about the love of Jesus Christ. The church received an award from the government for its work on the building. Revival is changing things in Cuba!

A Genuine Outpouring of Love

After the service there was an outpouring of love the likes of which I have never seen. All of our group were hugged and kissed by almost every member of the congregation. Men, women, or children, it did not matter. The three phrases most often heard were "We love you, God bless you, and Gracias (thank you)." As Christian love filled the air, tears of joy flowed freely. One man who shoved his hand at me, a hand callused from years of toil in the tropical heat, looked at me as the tears in his eyes rolled down the deep, weathered lines in his face. He simply said, "My brother in Christ." I, too, could not hold back the tears as I embraced my Christian brother knowing I would probably not see him again until we stood at the throne of God, while we as brothers waited for our Father to welcome us home. The two of us had come from very different worlds and did not speak the same language, but we shared the same faith in our

Lord and Savior, Jesus Christ. The political wrangling of our two countries seemed a million miles away. It appeared almost impossible that this beautiful island was poised, almost four decades earlier, to become the "OK Corral" of the twentieth century. Thank God it didn't.

The Pint-Size Candy Riot

After four hours in this church with its high-vaulted, two-story ceiling, no one really wanted to leave. It was as if we all wanted to make that very special day last as long as possible. Our team members then began handing out candy to the children. The same excitement that I've seen on the faces of American children showed on the faces of these Cuban children as they received their sweet treats. In what seemed like only moments, the word spread up and down the streets of Guantánamo and soon there were dozens of children everywhere. Only by ducking back into the church and being led through the back door to our waiting lunch averted a pint-sized candy riot. We were then escorted through the rear of the church to the adjoining home of the pastor.

Starting with a Home Chapel— Building to a Church

In Cuba, a permit for a church will only be given if the pastor lives on site. In many of the home chapels we visited on our trip, we discovered that I.C.M. first purchases an individual home for the pastor and his family. This allows the initial congregation to begin meeting in the front of the pastor's home. Once the church size justifies it, an adjoining building, in many cases, is purchased to expand the church, or a building permit is obtained, when possible, to construct a new building.

What An Impact for Thirty Dollars

It is very hard in Cuba to obtain a permit to move a church from its existing location. Therefore, part of the strategy used when buying homes for "home chapels" is to, when possible, purchase one with an adjoining piece of property, or a lesser quality building that can be renovated during the expansion process.

The cost to build churches in Cuba is insignificant by our standards. As difficult as it is to believe, the cost of a meal in a nice restaurant in the United States can, in Cuba, provide a building for a lifetime of worship for an individual member. With 200 members and a $6,000 budget, this breaks down to only thirty dollars per individual. Think about it: a lifetime of worship, a lifetime of praise, a lifetime of changing other's lives all for thirty dollars per member.

You Can't Describe the Ocean if You Have Never Seen It

I am reminded of the many times, from my adolescent years to today, when I have sat in a worship service and listened and watched as a missionary showed slides of a Third World country while telling of their many needs and asking for our mission dollars to be committed to that area. While I listened to the message, heard the words, and sometimes had the strings of my heart tugged upon by the pictures, it cannot hold a candle to actually being there. I encourage everyone reading this book to commit to joining I.C.M.'s ministry in placing churches not only in Cuba, but all around the world. There is no better way to be inspired than to go on a mission trip yourself. For more details, see our "Yes I Want to Help" form in the back of this book or visit our web site at www.CubaStory.com.

Thank You for Giving to the Lord

I am reminded of a song performed by the Christian recording artist Ray Boltz. The name of his song is "Thank You" and tells the story of a person arriving in heaven. People begin to approach from all sides saying, "Thank you. Thank you for all that you have done." The song continues with one person, who is thanking heaven's new arrival for giving his time to teach a Sunday school class, a class that told of the love of Jesus Christ and led a young boy—this person—to the Lord. A subsequent verse tells the story of a missionary in a Sunday morning service showing photographs that touch the hearts of one member. The song goes on to say that while he did not have the money to give, he gave anyway and because of those funds this person is now thanking him for his salvation that followed as a result of that gift. The refrain simply says "Thank you for giving to the Lord." I feel Ray's song should be our unofficial theme song of the evangelization of Cuba.

A Pebble in the Pond of Life

When you drop a pebble in a pond, you never know where the ripples will reach. When you honor your Lord and Savior, Jesus Christ, with a gift to one of these churches, you will never know where the ripples of that gift will reach. Our job is not to keep track of those who are touched, but simply to follow Jesus' instructions when he gave us the Great Commission. He said in Matthew 28:19-20: "Therefore go and make disciples of all nations baptizing them in the name of the Father and the Son and of the Holy Spirit, and teaching them to obey everything I have commanded you. And surely I am with you always, to the very end of the age." When someone is dying his last words are considered by most to be of the greatest importance. Even a court of law gives special consideration to the dying words of a man. As a man is about to be executed it is customary to give him a chance to say his last words. Jesus, knowing He was about to die, left the Great Commission as His last words of instruction to His disciples; they were to go everywhere and make more disciples. We may not all be evangelists in the formal sense, but we have all received gifts we can employ to help fulfill the Great Commission.

By the Numbers

One of the reasons that these buildings can be constructed for such a low cost is because, in Cuba, as in many Third World countries, a limited amount of currency is in circulation. Let's look at the numbers. At the time of this writing the Cuban peso is trading twenty to one to the U.S. dollar. This means the peso is worth about five cents U.S. The average Cuban earns twelve dollars U.S. per month, or 240 pesos. A highly skilled worker, such as a doctor, earns thirty dollars U.S. monthly—equal to about 600 pesos. Most prices follow a relationship to labor cost. For example, if the labor cost to make concrete is lower, the cost of the concrete will be lower. If we put one hundred dollars into a church, it will buy goods and services equal to a highly skilled worker's wages for three months. Subsequently, a small amount of currency can buy a great deal in these countries. This is true whether we are speaking about food, clothes, or building materials. Simply put, a dollar goes a long way.

Built with Their Hands and Hearts

Another reason we receive such a "bang for the buck" is that most of the work to build the church is completed by the congregations. It is the members who are building their church with *their* hands and *their* hearts. As we all know, much more enjoyment comes from anything in which we personally participate. The worship the congregation gives, with its labor, is the beginning of many years of worship to come.

The Pig

After saying our good-byes to the congregation at Getmo, we were then led to a long table on the back porch of the church where we sat down to a meal with the church leadership. A whole pig had been roasting on a spit over an open fire through the night. Once the ten-foot spit was removed, the pig was carved for

A great day for us, a bad day for the pig.

serving. With the juicy, roast pork we enjoyed Cuban black beans and rice, fresh tomatoes, onions, boiled potatoes and french fries, or *papas fritas*, deep-fried over the same open fire in a large black cast-iron pot. The meal was great but the fellowship was even better.

CHAPTER ELEVEN

On to Havana and Josh's Church

All Aboard the Sweat Box

After one more round of farewells to the Guantánamo church leaders, we were off for a quick stop at another construction site on the outskirts of Getmo before we began our four-hour ride to the airport in Holguín. We were to catch a flight, again on a twin engine ATR42, affectionately named by our group the "Sweat box." Two and a half hours after departing from the Holguín airport, and after one quick stop where we spent only forty-five minutes on the tarmac sweating profusely, we arrived in Havana, Cuba's capital.

Havana by Dawn's Early Light

To us, the city was a bit deceiving as our hired van drove through the capital in the wee hours of the morning. After two days spent in the more rural eastern Cuba, the multi-story buildings gave us a hint of a metropolitan city. This illusion,

Havana by dawn's early light. Cuba's buildings and infrastructure are crumbling after four decades of neglect.

however, could not survive the light of day. From the open breezeway outside our sparsely furnished room on the fifth floor of the Hotel Kohly, the rays of the sun rising over the Caribbean Sea exposed a city in dire need of repair.

Even so, in their run-down condition, these buildings brought back long forgotten images of beautiful Colonial-style architectural splendor. Ornate fancywork on the stucco fronts of the predominately two-story homes coupled with columns and ironwork showed painstaking craftsmanship rendered five or more decades earlier. At first, I questioned why any government could allow a capital city to fall in such disrepair. Then I am reminded of the order of current priorities. Cubans are first and foremost concerned with the basic necessities of life. They toil on a day-by-day basis to provide their families with food, shelter and clothing. After that comes transportation needs, gas for those lucky enough to own a vehicle and items we all desire to make our lives more comfortable and enjoyable. Simply put, paint and stucco falls several steps down on the scale of importance. Coupled with a lack of access to building materials and the ever-present need for government permits, the end result is a once stately metropolitan city reduced to a state of shambles.

Now to Josh's Church

Sunday morning my son and I, along with three other members of our group, journeyed through the old downtown section of Havana, or *Habana vieja*. Our destination was to visit the first church that we, as a family, built in memory of our son/grandson, Josh. None of the I.C.M. staff had visited this church, post-construction, so we did not know what we would find. It took some time to locate the church due to a lack of street signs and house numbers.

After circling and re-circling several blocks for over a half hour and asking directions from at least six bystanders, we finally stopped to discuss our strategy for proceeding. One in our party said, "Listen." We then heard the distant sounds of praise music. With that we began to trace the origin of that familiar Latin beat. As we followed the music, we soon located the only building in many square blocks of Havana which sported a fresh coat of paint.

Once stopped in front of the church, we piled out of our aging Volkswagen van. The pastor and several members of the congregation met us in front of the church. Although we had never met, there was an immediate kindred spirit shared for centuries by believers worldwide. The pastor led us through the long, narrow shotgun-style building. The first three rooms had been combined to make a meeting facility that can accommodate seventy-five worshipers if you stack them in carefully. This church, like all we've seen, is begging for room to grow. Only the size of the facility, we are told, limits the number of attendees.

(Top) This is typical of the neighborhood where Josh's church is located. In fact, this house is located directly across the street. (Bottom) Richard greeting pastor at Josh's church. The bright coat of paint is quite a witness in a country devoid of exterior mainte-nance in most of the buildings.

The Pastor's Home

While the congregation sang, our small party made its way to the rear of the building. Here in three small rooms was the pas-tor's living quarters. He, his wife and two young children were very proud to call this home.

The first room we entered was a combination living room and kitchen. It was small and old but very clean and well kept. To the left was a single bed, shared by his five-year-old son and seven-year-old daughter. At the end of the hall was a small closet approximately four feet wide and three feet deep. This closet had been converted to a makeshift office containing a single chair, a tabletop fashioned from an old door and shelves built to the nine-foot ceiling. Like most Caribbean residences, this home had a high ceiling to allow heat to rise. I was immediately struck by the fact that the weekly messages delivered to this congregation were prepared in such meager study facilities.

As we backtracked to the main room we looked at the second and last bedroom which was the sleeping quarters for the pastor and his wife. Very small, it contained a double bed that covered the floor with only two inches to spare. The width of the mattress covered half the doorway leaving only two feet to enter the room. Obviously, there was not room for a nightstand, a table or a lamp. No matter how small their home may seem by our standards, they were very proud of it. Through our interpreter we talked several minutes with the pastor about where the church has come from and where it is heading. The pastor then asked if any of us felt led to preach, and the congregation was ours. After the two days I had spent in Cuba, the Sprit-filled services I had attended and being here at this service to meet the congregation of the church we had dedicated to Josh, he did not have to ask twice. I was ready to preach!

Addressing the Church

The pastor introduced us to the congregation and with our interpreter I mounted the small tile-covered riser that served as a stage at the front of the small church and turned preparing to address the congregation. Suddenly the events that had brought together the lives in this room began to play through my brain like an old movie. I thought of how God had blessed our family with young Joshua. No matter how unlikely it may have seemed at the glorious occasion of his birth, here we stood in old Havana, *Habana vieja*, Cuba, with a new extended family. No matter how little sense Josh's death seemed to make two years earlier, I could see, first hand, in the faces of these people what a difference his young life had made. This church, these brothers and sisters in Christ, the children had all been touched in a special way by little Josh's life. I could not help but wonder as I looked into their dark eyes, who, through this church, had accepted our Lord and Savior, Jesus Christ into their heart. I wondered if they would know Josh in heaven. For some reason, I feel they will.

You Could Feel It

That warm, sunny Sunday morning you could feel the presence of the Holy Spirit in that small Cuban home chapel. For the next few minutes, I shared from my heart how excited our family and I.C.M. were to have the opportunity to partner with this church's growth. As the paddle fans swirled the morning air, my voice was being amplified over a small, tattered guitar amp, which rested on a handcrafted wooden shelf mounted about seven feet high. As I spoke, the people listened. Many sat on the edge of their seats as if that position would help them embrace each and every word our interpreter repeated in their native tongue. Many clutched their Bibles, some prayed, but in our own way we all worshiped Jesus Christ.

The Exchanging of Gifts

The highlight of the morning was presenting the congregation a framed eight-by-ten picture of Joshua with the words "In Memory of 1995–1998" written in Spanish at the bottom. I can assure you there were very few dry eyes in the room.

After the message I slowly stepped from the small stage and took my seat beside my son. We embraced and, without a word being spoken, both of us know that Josh would be happy. This was a fitting tribute to his short life. We hugged and cried softly as our friend and founder of I.C.M. Dois Rosser, laid his hands softly on our backs to provide comfort.

The pastor then took the few steps to the platform and in a cracking low voice he began to speak. His words made their way through our interpreter crossing the two languages and bridging

(Left) The pastor of Josh's church uses a closet for his study.
(Top Right) It is amazing that this entire building and renovation
was completed for only $3,500.
(Bottom Right) During the dedication services, we present a picture of Josh

many years of conflict between our two countries. He told of an
old Cuban tradition. "Our tradition dictates," he said as he
looked down almost afraid to make eye contact, "That when a
gift is given to you in love, you are expected to reciprocate with a
gift of equal value." He then reiterated that, "Cuba is a poor
country and ours is a poor church." He continued, "There is no
way we could ever give you a gift fitting to repay the one you gave
to us, our church." At that moment I wanted to say this is not our
gift. We were simply stewards of what God had given to us and
we were just passing His blessings along. But he had the microphone and so all I could do was sit and listen.

Faithful Forever

He continued to speak and finally broke down sobbing uncontrollably. I was curious as to why he was becoming so emotional. I then noticed that his right hand was cupping his left hand, and in his fingers he was twisting a small silver object. The pastor then said, "Ten years ago I married my wife. On that day I promised to be faithful to her forever." He went on to say that on their wedding day both had exchanged wedding rings, a sign of their faithfulness for a lifetime. Then he looked at me. Our tear-filled eyes locked and he said, "The only gift I have to give to you which would be fitting is my wedding ring," as he removed it from his hand and extended it to me in a gesture of presentation. "Today I gladly give this ring to you promising to be faithful to this church, just as I have promised to be faithful to my wife, for a lifetime." There were tears in every eye in that church but above all there was a quietness that had fallen over the church.

As the pastor held the ring extended toward me in his trembling hand, I stood to slowly walk to the platform. What should I do? What should I say? I did not want to take his wedding ring, but at the same time I did not want to offend my Christian brother, and the congregation as he made such an unselfish gesture. I bowed my head and asked God for the wisdom to have the right words. I then stepped to the podium and accepted the ring from the pastor.

Never Question His Heart

As I turned to face the congregation, I saw that all of them shared the pastor's pain and simultaneous pride. As I held the ring in my hand I said to the congregation, "I accept this ring in the Christian love that it was given." I continued with the congregation, "There will be times in the future that you will question this pastor, his motives, his determination, his actions, but never," I said, "should you ever question his heart." Then as I turned to the pastor I said to him, "Now this gift leaves me embarrassed. I have nothing to give back to you. I ask you to please accept this ring from me to you as a sign of my Christian friendship." He was tentative at first but then reached and accepted the ring from my hand. He was crying. I was crying. The congregation was crying. Never in my life have I experienced a moment so moving as that moment. I wonder if I would have had the courage to do what he has done, the unselfishness to give something as important as my wedding ring as a gift to repay another for their help in giving me a place to worship our Lord and Savior, Jesus Christ. My thoughts again returned to Josh and all the people his life has touched. How can I help but believe that all of this is part of the Lord's master plan.

Goodbye For Now

Much too soon it was time for us to bid farewell to our new friends. With hugs and handshakes, and after posing for one group photo, we reluctantly piled into our Volkswagen van. That afternoon, we visited four more churches or building sites. Everywhere we went people from the neighborhood flocked to their church just to thank us for being there. From shortly after sunrise to late in the evening, each day on our whirlwind trip through Cuba we rode an emotional roller coaster. We could not help but be thankful for what God has blessed us with, but we could also not escape the feeling of empathy for the pain that our brothers and sisters in Christ feel in this proud island nation.

His Plan—His Purpose

Today, more than ever in my life, I believe that God has a plan for all of us, if we will just listen and follow his will. After my grandson's death I made a promise that I would live my life to make a difference. I do not understand why I've been given nearly a half century of life, at this point, and my grandson had less than three years, but I do know, because of that little boy, I have a different outlook on life today. Because of Josh I have a closer walk with my Lord. After his death my pastor said to me, "God puts each of us here for a purpose and after we fulfill that purpose He takes us home. Today I feel that Josh's short life is still making a strong impact for the Lord's work.

CHAPTER TWELVE

The Last Night in Cuba

Our Last Night in Cuba

It was after 11:00 P.M. Sunday evening when we arrived back at Havana's Kohly Hotel. We were told that the government-owned bus would pick us up at 4:00 A.M. in front of our government-owned hotel for the twenty-minute ride to the government-owned Havana airport where we were scheduled to depart from Cuba at 7:30 A.M. on the government-owned airline for the United States via Cancun. I questioned why we must leave at 4:00 A.M. for what is only a twenty-minute ride to the airport. I was told the government not only owns everything but also makes all rules pertaining to everything they own. Simply put, the rules dictated that we would leave at 4:00 A.M. and it was not negotiable—comrade. I am certain that I would never survive in a Communist country.

Have You Seen My Sunglasses

Resigned to the fact that we had only four hours to sleep before reveille, my son and I climbed into our beds for our last short night's sleep, in Havana, Cuba. The lights had been out for only two minutes when my son said, "Where are my sunglasses?" Turning the light back on he stated, "I left them right here beside the bed today." Much too tired to discuss under which pile of clothes or luggage the sunglasses were probably hiding, I told him that we would find them during our packing, which would now begin in only three and a half hours. I pled, "Let's try to get some sleep, Shane." He reluctantly agreed and once again turned the light off. We now had only three hours and twenty-five minutes until our scheduled wake-up time.

The Call

At 1:30 A.M. the phone rang in Room 530 of the Kohly Hotel at the same decibel level as that of an oncoming freight train. Assuming it was our wake-up call I quickly retrieved the 1950s-style basic black receiver from its cradle. As I placed it to my ear, I was told that I should bring my passport to the lobby, that Policía Nationale Revolution (the national police) had "things" from my room. This of course got my attention and I mumbled something about, "Okay, I'll be there in a minute." I got out of bed. Shane asked, "What is going on?" At that point, I was unsure as to how to answer his question. I advised him, "I'm sure it's nothing, just go back to sleep." Putting on yesterday's pants and a T-shirt but still barefoot, I headed to the lobby wiping the too-little sleep from my eyes.

It's Got to Be a Joke

As I descended the five stories in the aging hotel elevator, I halfway expected one of my traveling companions to be laughing in the lobby when the doors opened. Much to my dismay as the door retract, standing about twenty feet from the elevator were six armed Cuban policemen. I quickly realized that this was no joke. In my mind I was thinking, "What items do they have from my room? What can that mean?" Obviously it meant they had been in my room. Who were "they"? The police, the military or was it government agents? What could they have found? I knew that I had checked my bags before I left the States. I had followed to the letter the rules on the information sheets given to us by the I.C.M. The instructions clearly stated to bring only prescriptions in their original bottles, no contraband, no mace. I'm sure that they could have found nothing. Wait a minute…except the handwritten journal I had been keeping.

My Journal

For some reason, the day I left the United States, I began writing a journal of my trip. This book is the result of that journal. As my mind went to the journal, I knew that I had been anything but complimentary of the Communist form of government. Did they have my book? How did they get it? They had no right to enter my room. Rights, oh yes, those were something that I had left in the United States four days ago.

Never Surrender Your Passport

As I slowly walked toward the six stone-faced policemen, I announced to them that I was Richard Parker. The first guard said sharply, "passport" with his outstretched hand palm up. As I gave him my United States passport, my ticket back to freedom, the picture ID that I have used to travel the world, the document that is littered with purple ink stamped by numerous countries, I saw the guard, much to my dismay, slide my passport into his top pocket. Wait a minute, this is a violation of the cardinal rule of international travelers. Never under any circumstance give up your passport, and above all do not give it up in a Communist country. I debated what my next course of action should be. Do I throw a fit and demand, "Give me back

The Policia Nationale Revolution (The National Police)

my passport." What if they will not give it back? My mind raced. Go to the U.S. Embassy. That's it, I will call the embassy. Wait a minute! We severed relations with Cuba in the early 1960s. THERE IS NO EMBASSY! I decided that I would simply keep the national policeman in sight, thereby not losing contact with my passport until I could surmise what this early morning inquisition was about.

What Did He Say?

Two of the policemen began speaking in Spanish. Of course I was unable to understand what they were saying, but I assumed it was about me. I asked one of the policeman, "What is this about?" He held the pointer finger of his right hand straight up in the air and nodded once at me. This universal sign for "just a minute" gave me even more cause for concern. Why could they not tell me why I had been summoned at 1:30 in the morning to the lobby?

Only 150 Minutes Left

My thoughts quickly went back to our scheduled time of departure. I became even more concerned. In only two and a half hours, our bus would arrive to pickup our team of seventeen and take us to the airport for our return trip. Would we be a group of seventeen or a group of sixteen returning to the United States?

I was concerned that no matter what this meeting was about, it would not reach a satisfactory conclusion in less than 150 minutes. My mind began to race between memories of the movie *Midnight Express* and the horror stories I had heard of Americans being held for no reason in foreign jails for weeks, months or even years. What could this be about? A few words that I wrote in my journal? I asked again, "Could you tell me what this is about?" Whether it was the communication problems or simply the police wanting to discuss the situation before I was made aware of the details, my question was again answered with the single index finger pointed skyward, as I was told again, "Just a moment."

Concern Turns to Fear

I was now moving from concerned to downright scared. My interpreter—that's what I need. I asked if I could call him and this time my question went completely unanswered. I decided that patience was the order of the day. After all, patience is a Cuban pastime. I've seen it in the lines of people waiting for bread, transportation, ration coupons—now it was my turn to learn the virtues of patience, and I needed to learn them very fast. Unfortunately, patience is an attribute that seems to elude me. The mind works in a strange way when you are under stress. I think of the cartoon of the two buzzards sitting on a branch near the desert. One looks at the other and the caption reads, "To heck with patience, I'm going to go kill something."

I knew that I should wait. But with each passing minute, I was more desperate to know why I was being held in the middle of the night by the Cuban National Police. I decided that if this kept up, I was not staying at the Kohly Hotel in downtown Havana, Cuba ever again. There goes that strange mind of mine again.

Thank God—You Speak English

Just about this time a young Cuban man, approximately twenty-five to twenty-eight years old, came from a side room. He said in perfect English, "Good evening, Mr. Parker." My initial reaction was, "Thank God somebody speaks English." That thankfulness was quickly replaced with my concern for what he was about to say rather than what language it was about to be said in.

I replied with a tentative hello and quickly asked, "What exactly is this about."

"We have some things from your room." I fought off the urge to ask, "How did you get anything out of my room without my permission?" but instead I gave a single word reply, "Oh!" mustering all the surprise I could in the hopes it would in some way help my case. Whatever my case turned out to be. The young man, who was obviously a front desk supervisor at the hotel, asked, "Mr. Parker, do you have a Palm Pilot?"

"Yes, I do."

"And a cell phone?" he asked.

My mind was racing, "There is no problem with owning a Palm Pilot and cell phone in Cuba is there?" There is no information in my Palm Pilot that should be objectionable to the Cuban authorities. My cell phone won't even work in Cuba. Why would they break into my room to hijack my phone and Palm Pilot? I'm not a spy. There are no national secrets in my Palm Pilot. I said, "Yes I have a cell phone."

I was still uneasy with where this conversation was leading. The young supervisor then said, "And are you also missing a camera?"

Missing? He said "missing." I liked the way the word "missing" sounded. For the first time this conversation sounded like the problem may not be centered around me.

"I'm not sure if I'm *missing* anything." Seeing a crack in the door I asked, "Why do you ask?"

He then reached over the front counter and retrieved my Palm Pilot, my cell phone, and my camera. He further asked, "Are these yours?" To which I replied with growing confidence, "Yes, they are."

At Last, The Truth

The hotel supervisor then explained that earlier that evening, before we returned to the hotel from our church visits, a hotel security guard observed a young Cuban man acting suspiciously. He approached the young man and questioned him. At the time the security guard had no way of knowing that the young man had broken into our hotel room and stolen the items which now lay on the front desk. The young man, after being questioned, had gotten nervous and shoved the cell phone and Palm Pilot under the cushion of a lobby chair and then walked into the courtyard and tossed the camera on a first-floor ledge.

Caught Red-Handed

This was a bad location for our young burglar to hone his illegal skills. In this state-run country foreign tourists are housed in specific hotels—both for security purposes, and I'm sure also to keep an eye on the comings and goings of the foreign guests. The government-owned Kohly Hotel had a small surveillance camera installed in the lobby ceiling facing the chair that the burglar had chosen to stash his ill-gotten booty. "Smile, you're on Candid Camera." The young Cuban man had been caught red-handed. The National Police were called, the man was arrested, and this brought us to the meeting being held in the wee hours of the morning.

The Handcuffed Young Man

It was only then that I noticed a young man sitting to the right with a handcuff firmly attaching his arm to the chair he was sitting in. Shortly, he was led to the parking lot and put in the back of a police car and driven away. One of the policemen then told me that they needed to take some pictures for the case. Obviously, I was agreeably relieved that it was not me being led to the Cuban calaboose.

The Evidence

A police photographer then took a series of photos of each item stolen. First the cell phone was placed on a table with a small piece of putty beside it. Then a small plastic #1 was inserted in the putty. The process was repeated with a #2 denoting the Palm Pilot. This process was repeated until all the items were photographed. Then four of the police, the photographer, and two of the hotel personnel accompanied me to my room to check our door to see how our young friend gained access to the room.

Go To Sleep—
The Police Are Just Passing Through

As the authorities walked through our room checking the doors and windows, my son woke up to find a room full of armed Cuban police at the foot of his bed. I simply said, "It's okay, son. Go back to sleep." Shane has never had a problem going to sleep. In another thirty seconds I heard snoring from under his covers. All I could think is, "I sure wish that was me sawing Z's."

After apologies are offered by the Cuban police, they bade me good night, all forty-five minutes left of it. Much too wired by the excitement to go to sleep, I began packing my clothes anticipating our departure from Cuba.

Heading Home

Our bus pulled to the front of the Kohly Hotel at 4:45 A.M. for our 4:00 A.M. pickup time. The bus was right on time—Cuban time that is. We all stumbled to our seats and began the first leg of our return trip. As the bus made its way through the cool darkness of the Cuban morning, we discussed the events of the previous night. One of my traveling companions offered a most fitting comment. "Well," he said, "it will make a great ending to your journal, won't it." I replied with a smile, "Yes, I guess, it will."

During our Cuban trip, I had become somewhat of a magnet for the jokes from my fellow travelers. I was always busy writing in my journal and now, in fact, I did have a great ending for my tour of Cuba.

Off Bus #1, on Bus #2

Our bus made its way through the streets of Havana in the predawn hours of that April morning. There was no traffic and very

Murphy's Law is alive and well in Havana.

few streetlamps to light our way. As if the island was throwing one last curve ball at us, within a matter of thirty or forty blocks, the bus simply refused to go any farther. The driver pulled to the side, examined the engine, called the headquarters and within fifteen minutes a new bus pulled up to the rear of our disabled aging vehicle. In minutes we transported our bags from aging bus #1 to aging bus #2. It only took another fifteen minutes to arrive at the airport where we were promptly deposited at the international gate.

Wheels Up—Again

After two cups of strong Cuban coffee, we made our way to the waiting aircraft. As I settled into my seat beside my son, I took a deep breath, laid my head back against the threadbare upholstery and exhaled a long deep breath. What a trip! All the preconceived ideas that I had when I entered Cuba had been replaced with a collage of memories—memories of the people, places and things I had seen in the last four days. I was about to make a journey just a few hundred miles in distance, but decades apart from Cuba.

As our airplane climbed into the morning sunlight, I looked out of the window at the last remaining Communist nation in our hemisphere. It seems as if forty years ago someone hit the pause button in Cuba. The entire country, the economy, the people, Cuba's entire forward motion went into the pause mode. I wonder what event it will take, how long it will be, before once again the play button is pressed and Cuba regains its forward motion.

EPILOGUE

Home Again, Home Again

Landing in the U.S.A. felt very comforting after my four days in a Communist country. Once we arrived in the international melting pot of Miami, we followed the "U.S. citizens only" signs, bypassing the hundreds of international travelers attempting to gain entrance to the world's leading capitalistic country. My son and I were taking the final leg of our adventure as we prepared to fly from Miami to the home of Shamu, Bugs Bunny and Mickey Mouse—Orlando, Florida.

With little more than a one-hour layover we both settled into the padded seats of the airport for our scheduled departure. In a few minutes, a group of yellow T-shirt-clad teenagers approached the gate next to ours. Their laughter reminded me of the children in Cuba as I heard their giggles of excitement. I guess kids are basically the same around the world. They share wide-eyed innocence and are full of expectation with their whole life ahead of them, while having no fear and no sense of mortality.

I began a conversation with one of their sponsors only to find that they are from an Orlando, Florida church. They were returning from a mission trip of their own, to Central America. The kids were outwardly excited and I couldn't help but eavesdrop on their teenage chatter. "Boy, that was great," one said, "Can you believe how they lived" added another, "Did you see that goat?" one said while laughing loudly. All in all they were having a great time. Then, one young girl in a much quieter, almost reflective voice said, "It's like, God has really blessed us so much. I am like, sooooo totally thankful." I couldn't help but echo her sentiments.

How Many More

I wonder in God's great kingdom how many groups and individuals are just returning or preparing to leave, following the Lord's Great Commission, by taking His word to every corner of the world. I was tired from our trip, but also wished we could stop in Florida only long enough to hug our families, get clean clothes and return to our friends in Cuba. There is so much work to do spreading the gospel of Jesus Christ. I wish I could take every friend, family member, co-worker and fellow Christian with me on my next trip. If they could only see the need, firsthand, they all would be more than willing to help. But how do I convey to them the need, the images I've seen and the experience I've had? I can feel the frustration that I'm sure the many missionaries I've heard since my childhood days, must have felt as they tried to share what they have experienced firsthand in only fifteen minutes of our worship service, armed with only twelve 35mm slides. You must experience this in person to truly feel it.

What Will Happen to Elian?

While resting on the plane for the last leg of our trip, my mind replayed the Cuban journey like a VCR. Play, fast forward, pause, rewind and play again. I then focused on the little six-year-old Cuban boy who remained in the eye of the custody storm. I wondered how his battle would end. Would he go home to Cuba with his father or stay in Miami with his great-uncle Lazaro's family?

I had no way of knowing that in only a matter of days the quiet of the Saturday morning after Good Friday would be shattered as 130 federal agents converged on the Gonzalez home in Miami.

The Raid

Associated Press photographer Alan Diaz, who was stationed at the house next door, would see the federal agents piling out of their vans and would quickly jump the fence and run into the Gonzalez home. In less than two minutes he would have snapped the dramatic photo that would become one of the defining photos of our time: the infamous shot of the boy's rescuer, fisherman Donato Dalrymple, crouching in the closet while holding Elian. Facing them would be a goggle-clad federal agent in body armor holding an assault weapon shouting, "Get down! Get down! Give us the boy!"

The Gonzalez family lawyers would be huddled around the table in the dining room, talking on the phone with Janet Reno's Justice Department, in what they would think was a last-minute negotiation. This negotiation would prove to be only a diversion for the raid that was about to happen. As eight agents dressed in riot gear burst through the front door, two other agents would jump the rear fence and subdue the family's security consultant with pepper spray, placing a shotgun to his right temple. After breaking through the locked master-bedroom door, Elian would be found in Dalrymple's arms with the boy screaming, "Que esta pasando? (What's happening?)" Within three minutes of entering the home, I.N.S. agent Betty Mills would carry the young, crying boy from the home. He would

(Top left) The infamous photo seen worldwide
(Top right) INS agent Betty Mills makes a dash with Elian
(Bottom) Elian with his father, stepmother and half-brother Hianny

still be clad in the white T-shirt, plaid shorts and white socks he was wearing while he lay on the couch in the living room with his great-uncle Lazaro. Agent Mills and Elian would be protected by two dozen additional I.N.S. agents as they would make a hasty retreat from the small two-bedroom, one-bath Miami house, which Elian has called home for five months. They would then speed away in a white van with tinted windows in the post-dawn light.

Elian Is United with His Father

Elian would be quickly whisked to a waiting helicopter, then to an eight-seat jet that the U.S. Marshals Service normally uses to transport criminals. The plane is part of a fleet know as "Con Air."

In the minutes following the raid, the melting pot of Miami would begin to boil over. The city that Reno herself described as "a community that is hurting" would begin to react to the raid. The Cuban-American community would vent its anger throughout the day in small protest groups, some setting fires and vandalizing.

On the plane I.N.S. agents would try to allay the boy's fears. They would tell him he was safe and going to see his father. He would be given both chocolate milk and Play-Doh on the trip. Child psychologists use Play-Doh to help children relieve stress by having something to squeeze.

At 9:30 A.M. Elian, after five months, would be reunited with his father at Andrews Air Force Base. Juan Miguel would later describe how he watched the raid on TV.

As of the writing of this book the custody battle still rages in the U.S. court system. Elian remains with his father, step-mother and half brother Hianny in a home outside of Washington, D.C. On June 1, 2000 the courts ruled the I.N.S. acted properly when it denied a hearing to Elian. This cleared the next to the last hurdle in the family's legal saga, setting up Elian's return to Cuba. Elian's great-uncle Lazaro is now appealing this latest court order. Legal experts state that if this appeal is not successful the young boy should be cleared to return to Cuba. We can all only pray that the scars of losing his mother, being lost at sea and the international battle for him, which has raged now for over half of a year, will soon heal.

If They Only Knew

Soon we were preparing to land in the Central Florida city of Orlando. The city was built, many say, by a mouse named Mickey. I looked out the window and could visualize below over a million people going about their everyday American lives. They are driving any car which they can afford (and some they cannot). They are going to work and going to stores—stores filled with merchandise that anyone can buy, no permit required, no ration coupons needed. I see housing developments with homes that cost 100 to 200 times more than the homes that I had just left. I see swimming pools from the air that are the rule, rather than the exception, in these American backyards.

I began thinking that one month's mortgage payment on most of these houses is more than the cost of building an entire home chapel in Cuba, chapels destined to give eternal salvation to many Cubans, dozens, maybe even hundreds over its lifetime. If I could just share this message of the need to the thousands of Christian families below, I am sure that they would help. But how can I do this, how can I get the message to those who need to hear it?

The Clan Arrives

Arriving at the Orlando International Airport, we were met by my wife Joan, my daughter-in-law Gale and our oldest grand-child, Brittany. With the group was the newest addition to our family, Beau Parker Cole. He is now almost ninety days old. Beau is Josh's little brother and I see Josh in his little face more every time I look at him. Beau could never replace Josh but this precious gift from God makes our loss a little easier to take. He gives that wonderful little crooked smile when he recognizes that it's his Pa that is holding him. "Thank you, Lord." I pray this simple quick prayer almost every time I hold him. I wonder what his life will hold. What will he become? A paramedic like his father? A businessman like his Pa? A pastor like his great-grandpa? Will he find a cure for cancer? Will he be a great inventor or just a good Christian father? How different would his life be if he were born four hundred miles to the south in the Island Nation of Cuba?

I am overwhelmed with love for my family, thankfulness for the many ways God has blessed our lives and a burning desire to give back to Him and His kingdom.

The one-hour ride back to the East Coast of Florida took us down the Bee-Line highway, a road named for its straight-as-a-rifle-shot construction. During the trip, I tried to relate to my wife and daughter-in-law the experiences we had in Cuba. My family members listened intently, but I could tell that they did not sense the full impact of our Cuban excursion. How could I transfer the emotion I was feeling to them?

If My Wife Would Just Welcome Me That Way

Arriving at our beachside home, I was met by Sarge the Wonder Dog. Sarge is a two-year-old beagle who thinks that I hung the moon. He ran in circles wagging his tail and howling his traditional welcome home message. Now, if I could just get my wife to give me the same welcome home. As I unloaded the luggage, I kept noticing all the "stuff" that we own: a beautiful home filled with the treasures of a lifetime, a garage filled with the gems and junk we can't seem to live without. I walked into the grandchildren's room, a room that has been fashioned for their entertainment, enjoyment and as bribery to make them desire to spend more time with their grandparents than their parents. As I looked in this room I decided that maybe we should call it the grandchildren's toy box. It has every toy imaginable crammed into toy boxes, stacked on shelves and hanging from the walls. The colorful tropical fish decor with its decoupage walls reminds me of the island, floating in the emerald waters of the Caribbean, we had just left. How many of those toys have not been touched for months? How many would never be touched again, except to be sorted through to find yet another very important toy of the hour? How happy would they make the children that I had shared my last week, and now my heart, with. I walked out back to our pool area, which is encircled with an array of tropical plants. The bougainvillea, bird of paradise and swaying palms took my mind back to the lush rural countryside of Cuba. I sat in my comfortable rocker facing the pool, leaned my head back and closed my eyes and again pondered the question: How do I share this feeling, this burning desire to help those on the island?

My Journal

My thoughts drifted back to my last night there, to the early-morning phone call by the Cuban National Police and my initial concern that quickly turned to fear. The worry that my journal was the culprit that had caused the problem. My journal! That's it! Maybe it will help me transfer the impact of the Cuban trip to others. I dashed to my luggage and retrieved the one hundred-plus pages of handwritten notes. I began to thumb through the hen scratches, reliving the past few days with each new page that I scanned. Then it hit me. Although I travel constantly, I had never kept a journal on a trip. Why, without even thinking it through, did I start writing this journal on the day that I left Florida? Maybe this was part of God's plan for me. Maybe the unplanned journal was written so that I would have a means of sharing with you what would ultimately become this book. Maybe God was using the circumstances of Josh's untimely death to touch my heart, send me to Cuba, pen this book and through it touch your heart. I cannot say what God has in His plan for you. I can barely follow the direction He is guiding me. But consider how the long string of seemingly unrelated events has brought this book into your hands. Maybe these events are not unrelated at all. Maybe He intends to speak to you through this book. Are you listening? Take a minute now to ask for His guidance.

You Must Take the First Step

I once heard a pastor say, "God tells you what He wants you to do. He then may not give you additional directions until you take the first steps to follow His original directions." We as imperfect human beings procrastinate. We all do from time to time. Could this book be God's way of telling you to take action in helping to evangelize Cuba? What if you just put it off for an hour, which turned into a day or a year or the rest of your life? I urge you *now* to ask God for His guidance in how you can lend a hand in building these much-needed churches across that island country. Maybe you would like to come with us on our next Cuban mission trip. See the following appendix to learn more about how you can participate. I know that God will bless you for your help.

May the Praise and Glory be to Him.

APPENDIX

The Reason for This Book

This book was written with the hope that I could share just a little of the feeling that a group of seventeen Christian men, including myself, experienced on a recent trip to the island nation of Cuba. The reason for our four-day trip was to help build church buildings for a number of Christian congregations on that beautiful Caribbean island. These churches are being built through the International Cooperating Ministries (I.C.M.). As of the writing of this book, I.C.M. has been successful in building over 102 churches in Cuba and having under construction over 902 churches worldwide. I.C.M.'s president and founder, Dois Rosser, is a shining example of a Christian businessman who is using what God has blessed him with to honor our Lord and Savior, Jesus Christ. A modest man who is quick to point out that this is God's ministry, not his, Dois has been an inspiration to me and thousands of others worldwide.

He and his family, through The Rosser Family Foundation cover all the annual administrative cost of I.C.M. As a result, 100 percent of the contributions given to the ministry go directly to building the churches. This then helps to fulfill the Great Commission given by our Lord in Matthew 28:19 when He said, "Therefore go and make disciples of all nations, baptizing them in the name of the Father and of the Son and of the Holy Spirit."

The Dollar Goes So Far

What is so amazing to me is how far a dollar goes in Cuba. The average church budget to buy the land, building, or complete needed renovations to an existing church, is about $8,000 per church. Many projects are as low as $3,000 - $5,000. Because the Cuban economy has such a small amount of currency in circulation, a dollar goes a great distance. I saw many churches with budgets of $5,000, which had active memberships of 250 people or more. The businessman in me cannot help but marvel at the impact made on lives for as little as twenty to thirty dollars per member.

The first church our family committed to build in Havana was in memory of my grandson, Josh, who passed away in 1998. We felt this church would both honor our Lord and Savior, Jesus Christ, while giving us, as a family, a tangible way to remember a little boy whose short life touched us all so deeply. The dedication service described in Chapter 11 was one of the most touching, life-changing experiences I have ever had the privilege of participating in.

Take the Next Step Now

Maybe you have a saintly mother, father or other loved one that you would like to honor by building a church in their name. I strongly encourage you to act on this. Don't put it off! The lives that will be touched and the impact it will have on you and your family cannot sufficiently be described in words. If you would like to talk to me personally about this or to obtain more details, please feel free to call me at our Bible-Based Money Management™ Seminar offices at 877-739-9908 or visit us at our web site at www.BBMMS.com and click the Cuba Story logo on the home page. You may also download this book in an e-book format at www.CubaStory.com. On both sites you will see many more photos of our Cuba trip. You may also e-mail me at info@bbmms.com.

Come to Cuba with Us

After reading this book, you may find that you would like to attend one of the mission trips to Cuba. To learn more about making a trip there with us check the above web sites or call the above toll-free number at Bible-Based Money Management™ Seminars.

You may feel a calling to attend a mission trip to one of the many other countries where I.C.M. is engaged in building churches. These countries include India, Vietnam, Russia, Ukraine, Uganda, Zimbabwe and many more. We strongly recommend that, if this is the case, you feel free to contact I.C.M. directly at www.ICMMBC.org or call them at 800-999-3892.

I hope this book will touch your life just a fraction of how the trip to Cuba touched mine. I would also ask you to join this ministry in helping build these churches that are so desperately needed. In the back of this book you will find the "Yes I Want to Help" form. I hope you will take four steps: 1) read this book; 2) make a pledge to the I.C.M. ministry; 3) pass the book along to another or download the e-book for someone else from www.CubaStory.com; 4) pray for our ministry and the wonderful people of Cuba.

We ask that you please not take the tithe dollars that you have already committed to your local church to support this ministry. This should be done as an over-and-above gift. We know God will bless you for your stewardship of the gifts He has blessed you and your family with.

PLAN OF SALVATION

As I finished writing this book and the proofing began I felt a nagging uneasiness. There was something missing but I could not put my finger on what it was. I finally realized that while our primary reason for building these churches in Cuba was to help win lost Cubans for Christ, there was nothing in this book to outline the simple steps necessary to accept Christ into your life. What if a seeker was to read this book and finish without knowing how to accept Jesus Christ as their personal Lord and Savior?

If you are not a Christian or if you are not sure of your salvation, I ask you to take a few minutes to read this plan of salvation. Follow the steps as outlined below. Stop and pray the prayer outlined below. If you want someone to talk to personally, you may call one of our staff members at Bible-Based Money Management™ Seminars at 877-739-9908. Unless you are certain that you have accepted the gift of eternal life stop and accept this amazing gift, a gift that is free for the asking.

1. **Admit that you need to be saved** – This sounds so simple, but this is where it all starts. Admitting you are a sinner does not mean you are worse than other people. God's Word tells us, "For all have sinned and come short of the glory of God" (Romans 3:23)

2. **Accept that you can not save yourself** – Just as a diabetic can not cure themselves, a sinner (and all of us are sinners) can not save themselves. We can not gain entrance to Heaven by doing good works. The Bible says, "For by grace are ye saved through faith: and that not of yourselves: it is the gift of God: Not of works, lest any man should boast" (Ephesians 2:8, 9)

3. **Jesus paid the price for your salvation** – Out of total love for you God sent his only son to die on the cross for your sins. This is the greatest of all gifts and it was given to you without you even asking for it. The most powerful verse in the bible has got to be John 3:16. "For God so loved the world, that He gave His only begotten Son, that whosoever believeth in Him should not perish, but have everlasting life". All you have to do to accept his gift is to admit you are lost and believe in Jesus Christ as your Lord and Savior.

4. **Now is the time to accept Christ as your Savior** – We can never know what tomorrow holds. We never know if there will be a tomorrow for us. His word further states; "Behold now is the accepted (right) time: behold now is the day of salvation" (II Cor. 6:2)

5. **Do you need someone to help you accept Christ?** – You do not need a preacher or friend to help you receive salvation. You simply must call on the Lord (pray) and ask for His priceless gift. "Whosoever shall call upon the name of the LORD shall be saved" (Romans 10:13)

6. **Only God can answer your prayer** – Pray this prayer; "God be merciful to me a sinner, and save me for Jesus sake. Come into my heart, Lord Jesus, and give me peace with thee" (Luke 18:13)

7. **What if salvation is not true?** – God cannot lie, His promise is given in His Holy Word; "In hope of eternal life, which God, that cannot lie, promised before the world began" (Titus 1:2)

If you were sincere and confessed that you were a sinner hopelessly lost and unable to save yourself and that only through believing that Christ dying on the cross to pay for your sins you are now saved, welcome to the family of Christ.

Now that you are saved what is next? What should you now do?

- In Romans 10:9 we are commanded to tell another person you have accepted Christ as you savior.
- Jesus said to be baptized. "Repent and be baptized, everyone of you (Acts 2:38)
- Begin reading your Bible. Start by reading John, Romans and Ephesians
- Begin praying daily. Begin with a prayer of thanksgiving for your salvation. Then pray for guidance in your new life as a Christian.
- Find a Church to fellowship with other Christians

Congratulations and I'll see you in Heaven!

YES I WANT TO HELP

There are a variety of ways that you can help International Cooperating Ministries achieve their goal of placing churches in developing nations all around the world. Use this form to indicate the type of assistance you are interested in giving. We will contact you with details.

❏ Yes, I would like to make a one-time contribution to International Cooperating Ministries in the amount of_____.

❏ Yes, I would like to begin making monthly contributions to International Cooperating Ministries in the amount of _____ monthly.

❏ I would like details on ordering _____ copies of *Cuba: A Story of Revival* in bulk for my church group or other organization.

❑ I would like details on having the author of *Cuba: A Story of Revival*, Richard Parker, come to my chruch or event for a speaking engagement.

❑ I am interested in attending a mission trip to Cuba (or another developing nation) with International Cooperating Ministries. Please contact me with details.

Name:_____

Organization: _____

Address: _____

City/State/Zip:_____

Phone:_____ Fax: _____

E-mail:_____

We know God will bless you for your stewardship of the gifts He has blessed you and your family with.

See order form at the end of the book.

BIOGRAPHY

In 1994 Richard Parker founded Summit Brokerage Services, took it public in 1998 and sold controlling interest in 2002. Today he is the CEO of Educational Seminars of America, a training and seminar company. He is a humorous and highly sought after platform speaker and trainer delivering numerous presentations annually in the financial industry, churches and organizations across America.

He has also authored *Family Wealth Strategies* and *Bible-Based Money Management™ Seminars*. Both are comprehensive educational and generic three-night seminars comprised of seven-an-a-half money management courses taught in colleges, universities, corporations and churches respectively across the country. With the Bible-Based Money Management™, Christian financial advisors teach Christian families and churches alike what the Bible says about managing their money from a Biblical perspective. These Christian instructors are committed to helping fellow believers and their churches more effectively employ the assets that God has blessed them with. Each year the Bible-Based Money Management™ Seminar is taught in hundreds of churches nationwide. The course has recently been translated into Spanish opening it up to millions more.

Richard is also the author of *The Perfect Practice* specifically geared to the Financial Services professionals. This book is specifically geared to financial services professionals. The book, along with his two-day training course entitled *Practice Masters*, several audio, video, and software programs, teaches other financial professionals techniques on how to more effectively manage their practice. As a Christian businessman, Richard strives to honor Jesus Christ not only in his personal life, but in his business life, as well.

He is married to Joan Parker and has two grown sons. Wayne is married to Melissa, and together they have one child, McKenna Pace Cole, five years old. Richard's youngest son, Shane, who accompanied him on the trip to Cuba, is married to Gale. They are the parents to nine-year-old Brittney Shane Cole and Richard's newest grandchild and namesake, Beau Parker Cole, now three years old.

Cuba: A Story of Revival
Order Form

Postal orders: Richard Parker
P.O. Box 33446
Indialantic, FL 32903

Telephone orders: (877) 739-9908

Website: www.cubastory.com

Please send *Cuba: A Story of Revival* to:

Name: _____

Address: _____

City: _____ State: _____

Zip: _____

Telephone: (_____) _____

E-mail address: _____

Book Price: $14.95

Shipping: $3.00 for the first book and $1.00 for each additional book
to cover shipping and handling within US, Canada, and
Mexico. International orders add $6.00 for the first book
and $2.00 for each additional book

Fax Order Form to:
321-728-0213
or
contact your local bookstore